KEY MOMENTS IN ESPIONAGE

ABOUT THE AUTHORS

Piper Bayard is an author and a recovering attorney with a college degree or two. Jay Holmes is a fifty-year veteran of military and intelligence field operations, as well as a military and intelligence history scholar. His experience spans from the Cold War fight against the Soviets, the East Germans, and the various terrorist organizations they sponsored to the present Global War on Terror. Piper is the public face of their partnership.

Bayard & Holmes pen nonfiction books on espionage tradecraft and military and intelligence history, as well as fictional international spy thrillers. They are the authors of *SPYCRAFT: Essentials* for writers and espionage enthusiasts, and their fictional thrillers are known for authenticity of tradecraft. Their current focus is their Apex Predator spy thriller series.

When they aren't writing or, in Jay's case, busy with "other work," Piper and Jay are enjoying time with their families, exploring back roads, talking foreign affairs, laughing at their own jokes, and questing for the perfect chocolate cake recipe.

To receive notices of upcoming Bayard & Holmes releases, subscribe to the Bayard & Holmes Covert Briefing. You can contact Bayard & Holmes at their website BayardandHolmes.com, at @piperbayard on Twitter, or at their email, BayardandHolmes@protonmail.com.

KEY MOMENTS IN ESPIONAGE

SPY SHIPS, INTELLIGENCE FAILURES, & THE
COLD WAR ERA

KEY HISTORY
BOOK 2

BAYARD & HOLMES

Shoe Phone Press
2770 Arapahoe Road #132-229
Lafayette, CO 80026

In memory of L. Gillis Day

Beloved father, grandpa, friend, and

teacher of monks

CONTENTS

INTRODUCTION

In the first book in our Key History series, *Key Figures in Espionage,* we studied a variety of figures in espionage who inform us on the heights and depths of the human spirit. In this book, *Key Moments in Espionage,* we glean what we might from that fickle illusionist called "history" by looking at a diverse collection of historical moments in espionage.

Every true student of politics, foreign affairs, and espionage knows that the study of history is crucial for understanding the dynamics of the issues that face us today. Current events were not born in a vacuum. All that has come before is happening now, still unfolding in an unbroken cycle.

Battles and triumphs are thrown down by our ancestors and picked up by our children, to be replayed as each new generation faces the same challenges that have always faced humanity: the quest for survival, the quest for resources, the quest for security, and, on a deeper, more personal level, the driving hunger that most individuals experience for relevance and legacy. As a result, it is impossible for countries and their intelligence communities to respond to the shifting currents of global dynamics without an understanding of the past from which they spawned.

However, this necessity presents a paradox. While understanding and interpreting history is essential to comprehension of the present, the facts of history are frequently impossible to discern with complete accuracy. That is because all history is written by humans, and humans have agendas.

Humans, by our very nature, control the dissemination of information to our own advantage, whether it's the seven-year-old explaining why they ate their sister's cookie or the world leader explaining why protecting their own citizens required them to invade their neighbor, who just happens to have massive oil reserves. As a result, we, Bayard & Holmes, have literally seen critical events, some of which involved our personal knowledge, disappear from the collective memory before our eyes, to be replaced with silence, spin, or outright lies. Revolutionary uprisings, gun battles, weapons caches of despotic dictators, etc., have been scrubbed from the world's collective memory as various politicos, in conjunction with corporate and media moguls, cherry pick the information the public receives according to what best serves agendas.

No, we are not promoting nefarious conspiracies. True conspiracies involve a specific meeting of the minds, and throughout history, they rarely include more than a handful of people. Almost always, what people broadly refer to as "conspiracies" are, at their foundations, nothing more than a collection of diverse individuals, organizations, or societies with aligning self-interests acting on their own behalf. When the self-interests of Big Politics, Big Media, and Big Business dovetail, "truth" and "facts" are modified or erased on a worldwide scale to suit the agendas of the moment. What's left after these modifications and omissions becomes what most people blithely refer to as "history."

This is no recent phenomenon, though it is made somewhat easier with the internet. Behind every internet posting is a human with an agenda, and that agenda is almost never to provide objective facts. The people who control the process of information dissemination are the people who control the past, and those who control the past shape the present and lay the paving stones to the future. Thus, controlling the stories of our collective past is a form of power.

Yet beneath the power-hungry agendas, clumsy misinterpretations, honest mistakes, and outright lies, actual facts do exist, waiting like a pirate's treasure for that dedicated hunter or serendipitous fortunate to unearth them. For the espionage professional, it is essential to seek out those facts, no matter how unpleasant or inconvenient to the seeker's own human biases and agendas. In this book, as in all of our nonfiction books, we have done our best to do exactly that, at times actively hunting the treasure, and at times experiencing the fortunes of serendipitous discovery.

The style of the Key History series is narrative nonfiction, and most of the chapters included first appeared in our Bayard & Holmes articles published on our Bayard & Holmes website and on the global Social-In Network. We have collected these articles into three volumes, *Key Figures in Espionage, Key Moments in Espionage,* and *Key People & Wars.*

The information contained in these books has been gleaned from open sources, both domestic and foreign, and foreign and domestic government documents that we deem to be reliable, and personal experience. We openly admit that we are subject to the same obfuscation that plagues all historians and espionage professionals who must daily make decisions without full knowledge, so where the facts are impossible to discern, we present the alternate theories that we find either credible or interesting. At times, we let you know which ones we favor due to our own agenda, which is simply to discover and discern actual facts.

If we state something as a fact, it is because we have verified it through multiple sources that we consider to be reliable. Unlike mainstream media, if we state opinions, we make it clear that we are stating opinions and not facts.

And who are we to write this book? Piper Bayard is an author and a recovering attorney who has worked daily with Jay Holmes for over a decade, learning about foreign affairs, espionage history, and field techniques for the purpose of writing both fiction and nonfiction. Jay Holmes is a fifty-year veteran of military and intelligence field operations, as well as a history scholar. Because Holmes is covert, Piper is the public face of their partnership.

In this volume, *Key Moments in Espionage*, we explore the history of spy ships, various great intelligence fails, and a few select aspects of the Cold War Era.

It is imperative to effective spycraft that critical information about developing situations be relayed before it becomes irrelevant. Before that critical information could be relayed across telegraph wires, telephones, or the internet, it had to be physically carried, and when it comes to physical transportation, waterways have been essential since Ogg the Caveman first grabbed hold of drift-wood and floated downriver.

Ships not only provide transportation, they also give us a means to physically observe the workings of our friends and enemies around the world. Thus, spy ships have always been essential to espionage. In the first section of this book, we take a look at how spy ships have been employed over the course of history, with a special focus on the USS *Liberty* and USS *Pueblo* incidents during the latter half of the twentieth century.

Alas, communicating critical information is only one part of the espionage equation. Just as important is what becomes of that information once it reaches its destination. We would love to say that it's only politicians that screw things up when it comes to handling information, but since intelligence work is all about the facts as they are and not the facts as we wish they were, we must acknowledge that the most educated, experienced old spooks and military veterans can still make mistakes, and sometimes big ones. However, since success is always built on failure, it is useful to study some of the great intelligence failures that history has to offer. Hence, in our second section, we look at some great intelligence failures and the lessons that they teach.

We then focus on a few aspects of the Cold War Era. Throughout history, espionage has been used to inform political and military leadership, often for the purpose of conducting ground wars. The Cold War, however, was all about using espionage to minimize the scale of ground wars. As a result, espionage was the central player in the latter twentieth century battle between Western capitalist democracies and the communist Soviet Union and People's Republic of China. In these chapters, we explore some aspects of the power of flight during the Cold War Era, as well as some battles that were not so obvious. We also put a spotlight on the man who used the Cold War chaos to propel himself to riches and power, and who is still a prominent player today.

Join us now as we sort through the clues from our collective past and piece together a bit of the picture that we call our history.

SPY SHIPS

———

HISTORY OF SPY SHIPS

The Golden Age of Spy Ships

The US Navy Comes of Age

Spy Ships in the Civil War

Spy Ships in WWI and the Price of Ignoring Intelligence

Spy Ships and the Path to WWII

Cold War Spy Ships

Soviet and Russian Spy Ships

Chinese Spy Ships

———

TWO PROMINENT SPY SHIP INCIDENTS

The USS *Liberty*

The USS *Pueblo*

1

SPY SHIPS

IF FISHING IS THE OLDEST MARITIME PROFESSION, AND TRADE IS THE second oldest maritime profession, then spying is likely the third. As early as 4,500 BC, sailing vessels plied trade routes in the Mediterranean Sea and the Indian Ocean. Once trade ships gained access to foreign kingdoms, the respective kings and their military councils were doubtless anxious to hear any information brought back by sailors. Just as the kingdoms sending forth the trade vessels were eager to obtain news from foreign ports, the local potentates and merchants in those faraway places were just as anxious to know about the kingdoms the sailors called home. Hence, spy ships were born.

It's not hard to imagine ancient sailors far from home tanking up on local brew and being loose-lipped with seductive members of the "oldest land profession" who were spying for the local kingdoms. If we could time travel, it would be fun to compare the lines used by ancient booty spies with the lines used by modern booty spies. Since people are people, and times change but people usually don't, those lines would likely be quite similar.

By 1,000 BC, the Greek maritime nations had organized spy ship operations that were conducted by full time professionals. They employed regular paid spy teams to sail merchant routes, and they used trade activity as a cover for spying rather than as a primary economic activity. At times, those spy ships would pose as local fishing vessels to approach foreign shipbuilding operations and ports. That way, they could gain a sense of what neighboring navies might be doing. That and other types of Greek maritime intelligence gave the Greeks advanced warning of Persian invasions in both 492 BC and 480 BC.

The Romans took the art of spy ships to an even higher level than the Greeks. By 500 BC, Roman merchant sailor-spies, as well as spies on a few dedicated spy ships, reported to a well-organized intelligence agency within the Roman government. Roman maritime intelligence operations even included landing spies on foreign shores to travel inland to collect information. For the Romans, such seaborne spy operations played an important role in the conquests of Egypt and Britain.

However, Roman intelligence operations suffered the same vulnerabilities that all intelligence operations suffer—they weren't perfect. For example, in 214 BC, Rome's intelligence networks failed to discover new Greek war machines built in Syracuse. That lack of intelligence contributed to the failure of a Roman naval attack on that city. Imagine what a few well-disguised Roman sailors might have learned if they had gained access to Syracuse and observed the Greek construction teams at work?

The Greeks, on the other hand, were a bit more on the espionage ball, and a few skilled Greek booty spies had done their work well. The Greeks knew enough to arm Syracuse in time to damage and sink Roman ships before they could land troops.

As the Roman Empire perfected its spy ship techniques, other kingdoms did the same. By the time of Christ, trade ships and fishing vessels plying the Red Sea, the Arabian Sea, the Indian Ocean, the Black Sea, and the Pacific continued to act as spy vessels for maritime nations. Governments assumed most of the world's trade ports, including the small ones, were filled with spies posing or doubling as traders, fishermen, shipwrights, and merchants. In some cases, nations like Oman and Persia carefully crafted disinformation and had double agents leak it to the visiting ships.

Other nations, such as Japan, grew weary of all of the maritime intelligence activities against them and became more isolationist. In 550 AD, the Japanese Emperor Kinmei heeded the advice of his war lords and restricted port visits and fishing activities in coastal waters by vessels from Korea and China. Local coastal villages began routinely reporting sightings of foreign vessels to the nearest war lords.

A few hundred years later, on the other side of the world, Viking raiders in Northern Europe realized that cruising down the coast until they found a port to pillage gave advance warning to the locals to muster their forces. This made the Vikings vulnerable to counterattacks at sea before they could make landfall. Also, as sensible plunderers, the Vikings did not want to raid military strong points with well-garrisoned castles, as they found that attacking the wrong ports at the wrong times ended in them being the main entertainment at French or British barbecues. As a result of these factors, the Vikings wised up. Starting in 793 AD, they began intelligence-gathering operations and used the information gleaned from sailors on trade vessels and other ships to plan their attacks on the coasts of Ireland, England, Scotland, and France. Their widespread success was due to these successful intelligence operations.

A couple centuries after that, England and Normandy also made extensive use of spy ships and maritime espionage, and at least one great battle between those two countries turned on intelligence, or the lack thereof. In August of 1066, King Harold of England had just defeated Harold of Norway at Stanford Bridge when he heard word of yet another "man who would be king" on his shores. King Harold hurried down to Hastings to defend his kingdom. If his supporters in London had known about William of Normandy's growing forces in time, they could have mustered adequate local levies to support King Harold at Hastings. However, the king did not receive intelligence on the gathering ships in Norman ports. As a result, King Harold had to march south from London before the bulk of his army had returned from Stanford Bridge. He lost his kingdom and his life to the Norman invader at the Battle of Hastings, and William of Normandy became known as William the Conqueror.

In time, William the Conqueror and his heirs became too "Anglicized," and their claim on the Normandy homeland was challenged by the French and Norman dukes. However, because the French and Norman naval intelligence operations failed to gather information about naval forces in British ports, the English were able to repeatedly invade the French coast at great annoyance and cost to the French throne and various Norman dukes. In contrast, the British, perhaps having learned from King Harold's mistakes, remained more meticulous in their spy ship efforts against the French, allowing them to land armies in undefended areas of France on multiple occasions.

One might wonder how could the French could possibly have failed to know what was happening in British ports. After all, some French courtier no doubt at some point observed, "I can see England from my house."

We share in your bafflement. Oddly, for all the repute of French prostitutes, we know of no successful efforts by French booty spies in British ports. Stranger still is the fact that the French and Norman dukes did not properly employ their own spy ship tactics that had worked well for them on other occasions, and would work well for them in the future.

We ascribe this failing to the mixed, confusing, and often side-swapping nature of the French chain of command. Due to disorganization and defections, no one on the French side of the channel took responsibility for keeping an eye on the British. One thing that the French knew and usually ignored about the British was that they would have to gather in force in ports and cross the English Chanel to land armies in France, but because of that "it's not in my job description" factor, French and Norman intelligence organizations were not well organized.

French failure to use maritime intelligence to predict the various attacks from the British usually allowed the British to avoid facing a united French army. As a result, the British gained local control over French and Norman garrisons. In time, however, the French got their act together, and in 1453 they defeated a force of invading Englishmen who were allied with momentarily anti-French Gascons at Castillon.

After that, the English throne turned its attentions inward on England and northward toward Scotland. England avoided most continental entanglements while enjoying the great English tradition of forming up teams of dukes to kill Englishmen fighting for other teams of dukes, while both sides claimed to be defending honor and the rightful heir du jour to the throne. On those days that they were not killing or being killed by Scots or Irish, the English vented their internal blood-lust effectively and gave these wars cute names like "The War of the Roses."

Likewise, the French throne, now slightly more secure from external threats, focused on the ancient French tradition of political infighting, keeping French rulers busy with the business of killing other Frenchmen. Fortunately for France, Spain was also busy with its 742-year-old tradition of trying to kill enough Moors to reclaim Spain.

One might assume that with such full agendas, the major European powers would be too busy for much spy activity. However, in their states of expensive and bloody preoccupation, it was as important as ever for all of them to remain informed about foreign naval and port activities. Also, both Spain and Portugal began looking outward to foreign shores, bewitched by the prospect of future conquests. Thus the world entered the golden age of spy ships.

2

THE GOLDEN AGE OF SPY SHIPS

BY THE 1400S, NATIONS AROUND THE WORLD HAD ACTIVE SPY SHIP operations. At the very least, those operations garnered information from seafarers in order to bolster their defenses against naval strikes or to support their own happy internal blood baths. Exploration and conquest were also strong motivators during that time period, and both capital ventures and governments were keen for information from abroad.

In 1432, Gonçalo Nuno Cabral of Portugal fanned these flames of exploration by discovering the Azores Islands, and sixty years later, an immigrant from Italy named Christopher Columbus had the audacity to approach Queen Isabella of Spain and request financing for a round-the-world sea journey. Columbus pointed out to the Spanish Monarchy that an established sea route to India would save the Spanish from having to undertake the usually-suicidal overland route to the Far East.

Not coincidentally, when Columbus sailed for "the Indies" in August of 1492, Spain had just completed its 781-year war against its Islamic occupiers. The nearly eight hundred years of intermittent war and political maneuvering had forged Spain into a culture of military toughness and political flexibility. It also left the warrior class and nobility of Spain restless and looking for a good fight. Columbus found them one.

When Columbus announced that he had found a route to India, which he thought he had, Spain was in a unique position to exploit that valuable bit of maritime intelligence. She had a large pool of people willing to sail across an ocean and conquer any "Indians" who were unable to see the beauty of Spanish Christian baptism and economic control. Columbus's discovery of vast and mostly fertile lands occupied by "Indians," who were busy acting like Europeans and everyone else of the time by killing and enslaving each other, set off a wave of exploration and conquest in the Western Hemisphere.

Spain's neighbor, Portugal, also had expansion projects in the works. Portugal had gotten a jump start on world exploration with journeys down the west coast of Africa in hopes of eventually reaching the same precious Indian ports. In 1498, a Portuguese reconnaissance made up of four ships reached Calcutta. Lead by Vasco De Gama, they had finally found the sea route to India that had eluded Columbus. De Gama's sea route to India lit the fires of exploration and conquest to the East.

As a result of Columbus's and De Gama's ventures, Spain, Portugal, England, France, and The Netherlands quickly established trade stations and colonies in the New World and in Asia. The evolving map of the New World held vast opportunities for wealth, and any nation that wanted it needed three things to get that vast wealth. They needed enough naval strength to reach and return from distant shores across contested waters. They needed intelligent and intrepid explorers to disembark from those ships to acquire that wealth by trade or conquest, and they needed good intelligence. During that cyclone of conquest and trade, the knowledge that any and every seaman might hold became more valuable than ever. Merchants, as well as naval crews, were expected to acquire as much information as they could from any coast they spied and every port they visited.

It was common during the 16th, 17th, and 18th centuries for ship captains to view intelligence collection as a primary part of any seaborne mission. The most valuable thing that an alert merchant crew could bring back to Europe was key information that would enable future trade or conquest. Frequently, these ships also carried travelers who were on spy missions for a European throne or a major trading house.

We pause a moment to imagine what it felt like to enter a pub in a Caribbean port. We would have to wonder who all the visitors where and what allegiances they held on that particular day. Which country or company did they represent, if any? Were they pirates? Who were the other spies in the room? What ships were they sailing on, and where were they going? One bartender and a well-managed team of skilled booty spies in one of those Caribbean ports could have run a lucrative intelligence operation, and they often did. The atmosphere was no doubt as tense as it was in areas of the Tangiers Casbah, the Hong Kong red light district, or particular cafés on the Champs Elysées in Paris during the height of the Cold War. Spy ships were at their prime.

3

THE US NAVY COMES OF AGE

ALL OF THIS EXPLORATION AND COLONIAL EXPANSION WAS BOUND TO cause conflict and create new nations, but before the first shots of the American Revolution resounded at Lexington and Concord, the Colonies gathered information via American merchant ships and whalers. Ascertaining British naval strength and a general sense of their deployments around the globe was easy enough, but as the Revolution progressed, it became more important for the budding United States to know where British war ships and troop transports were destined.

American spies did their best to obtain this information in the ports of England and in the beds of English leaders. However, British naval officers and the British Admiralty proved to be tough, well-disciplined targets. A British officer who might be willing to accept the affections of a pretty young stranger would often remain silent about his work. Sometimes, ship fitters and the merchants who supplied them were more rewarding targets.

Vessels returning information to the American colonies from Great Britain had to make sure that information reached those Western lands faster than the British could. To move information and spies back and forth across the Atlantic, the American colonials used a class of ships known as "packet ships," the earliest examples of which were modeled after small, fast mail ships. During the American Revolution, packet ships remained an important part of intelligence and communication for and in the American Colonies. Moving a piece of information from Charleston to Boston by land took several weeks, but by sea, when the winds were favorable, a message could be moved in a few days.

When British ships anchored in American harbors, Americans kept them under surveillance from land, and cargo boats and fisherman could approach them. Since the British had to assume that any given colonist was a loyal British subject until proven otherwise, they remained vulnerable to close surveillance any time they dropped anchor in an American harbor or tied off at an American dock.

The Rhode Island Assembly founded the navy on June 12, 1775, and the first book of Rules for the Regulation of the Navy of the United Colonies of North America was published November 28, 1775. It was a sparse navy, and its operations were not well documented during the American Revolution, but it transported intelligence agents back and forth between America and European countries. The few naval vessels and privateers under American colonial flags also reported on any intelligence they could pick up in Caribbean and European ports concerning politics, rumors, all military dispositions, the British military in particular, disposition of British naval troop ships, and anything concerning the British government. Any Navy ship was then, and currently still is, an intelligence gathering apparatus to varying degrees.

After the American Revolution, the US Navy all but disappeared except on paper. Sadly, we Americans assumed that, given our distance from the centers of European powers, we need not bother to operate a regular intelligence system to keep abreast of foreign developments. This isolationist attitude generally served us well, but it did nothing to support the US merchant fleet or the sizable whaling fleet. Without those seafaring enterprises, the US economy would have been even more fragile than it was for the first fifty years of its existence. Also, while most Americans were happy with their new-found independence, that same independence meant that Great Britain and her leading navy no longer protected US ships. In fact, the British Navy now became a menace to US ships.

In the United States, whalers and merchant carriers had to care about foreign naval and political developments, as well as pirate operations. Whalers reached farther across the oceans in search of the richest hunting areas, and running into the wrong foreign naval vessels could mean the loss of their ships and imprisonment or impressment of their crews into foreign service.

Other modern nations maintained no illusions about the importance of naval power and naval intelligence. Those nations maintained standing navies to insure their ability to trade over the seas. Great Britain, in particular, improved its navy with the quality of its ships and the training of its crews. As part of their efforts, the British maintained a regular structure for collating and disseminating the intelligence gathered from all of their ships. This process provided British ships with better information, resulting in lower losses to pirates and foreign navies.

But the US could not stay alone in its corner of the world forever, and its carelessness about intelligence led the Barbary states in North Africa to conclude that US merchant vessels were easy pickings. In 1801, the Libyan, Tunisian, and Algerian coasts had long been controlled by pirates. The pirates left British and French ships alone because they had glimpsed the British and French navies. They were not crazy. However, since there was almost no US Navy, the pirates took any and every US ship they wanted, kept them, and ransomed the US sailors.

Also in 1801, President Thomas Jefferson made his famous "we won't deal with terrorists" speech. A foolhardy young US Navy lieutenant by the name of Stephen Decatur took a ridiculously small force of ships and men to North Africa to enforce a "No Pirates Zone." The Pasha laughed, France laughed, and England, having the biggest and best navy, laughed the loudest. The King of Spain, on the other hand, said, "Don't laugh. I know these people. These Americans are trouble."

Decatur had the foresight to bring two important things with him. He brought Marines. They don't laugh. Ever. And he brought some hard-drinking Redsox fans from south Boston. Between the deadly Marines and fourteen years of nonstop chanting of "the Pasha sucks," the pirates wisely gave up. In 1815, the pirates signed a treaty agreeing to only pick on the English and the French. Decatur, in his farewell speech to Libya said, "Don't ever piss us off again. Next time we will bring carriers and even more Marines." Libya believed that for a long time.

In 1812, the United States grew tired of the British Navy's habit of impounding its merchant ships and impressing US crews into British service. Since the United Kingdom was busy fighting Napoleon and his allies, the United States thought it could mount operations against the United Kingdom's Canadian colonies, and that Great Britain would quickly relent. Unfortunately for the United States, by 1815, the United Kingdom was getting the upper hand over Napoleon's forces. It responded to the annoying Americans with increasing energy and resources. Fortunately for the United States, though, commerce and profit ruled the day, and the British reminded themselves that sending armies to the United States would be expensive. The greatest urgency for both the United Kingdom and the United States was to sign a peace treaty and resume trade.

During the War of 1812, the United States made great efforts to man and sail fast ships into British waters and harass unguarded British areas. In the process, those ships gathered as much intelligence as possible. The British, however, didn't bother. They already knew enough about our capabilities to concentrate adequate British naval forces wherever they wanted and seal off any American port that they chose.

After the Treaty of Ghent ended the War of 1812 in February of 1815, the US public returned to its isolationist stance within a short time, probably around ten minutes. However, for the merchant class and the US government, the war had a huge impact on their outlook. They never wanted the United States to be at the mercy of foreign navies again. The United States would forevermore operate a navy, and in the 1800s, that navy remained closely allied with the US merchant community. Intelligence began to flow in a more organized fashion to Congress and the Cabinet.

By 1845, the US Navy was a force to be reckoned with. During the Mexican-American War, US merchant vessels and ships under various flags made port calls for routine trade and collected adequate intelligence about Mexican port defenses. The US Navy used that intelligence, along with intelligence gathered by agents on land, to take and hold critical Mexican ports. This enabled US Army troops to land at Veracruz, Mexico for an expedition against Mexico City. (See *Key People and Wars*).

By 1852, most of Congress embraced the notion of US ships spying against foreign nations as a routine matter for any modern nation. In a major break with normal US isolationist foreign policy, based on intelligence gathered by US trade ships, Commodore Mathew Perry received orders to take a fleet of four US war ships to Japan, a country even more isolationist than the United States. Perry showed up in Japan in 1853 and demanded a trade agreement with that country. With Perry's arrival in Japan, the US Navy had come of age. Japan was a witness to that, and, in turn, began to question its own isolationist strategy. Japan began to build its own deep sea navy.

The US Navy has never lost sight of the critical role that intelligence plays in establishing and maintaining US trade with foreign nations. Congress has returned to a far more isolationist stance at times, but no US Navy vessel has ever again left port without her captain understanding that intelligence gathering is a basic responsibility of every US naval ship.

4

SPY SHIPS IN THE CIVIL WAR

MATHEW PERRY'S EXPEDITION TO JAPAN RESULTED IN OPENING UP trade in 1853 and had a major impact on US political and economic thinking. Previously, most Americans had taken a parochial view of the US economy. The United States was still a nation with a vast frontier, and the public lived with the expectation of discovering new resources within its own borders. After Perry's expedition, Americans increasingly subscribed to a more international view of economics. One of the effects of this new, broader view was that Congress and the taxpayers became more willing to tolerate the expense of maintaining a real navy capable of long-range operations in contested waters. As a result, in December of 1860, when South Carolina seceded from the Union, she was seceding from a Union that had a strong, modern navy with well-trained naval officers and experienced sailors and Marines.

Generally, we point to the Confederate shelling of Union-occupied Ft. Sumter on April 12, 1861 as the first shooting incident of the American Civil War. However, the shooting had actually started at Ft. Sumter on January 9, three months earlier, when

Confederate forces fired on the US merchant ship *Star of the West* as she brought supplies to the fort.

This January incident was emblematic of some important strategic differences between the Union and the fledgling Confederacy. At that time, the Confederacy had little industry and a largely rural population. It had slaves and produced cotton, a nearly worthless product unless they could export it to Europe. Until the Civil War, the South was disproportionately represented in West Point, and it had filled more than its share of billets in the US Army. This gave the South a strong corps of experienced, well-trained army officers for her infant army, but few naval assets. The Union had more industry and only four slave states, which were Kentucky, Maryland, Delaware, and Missouri. In 1861, the US Navy was disproportionately populated by officers and crews from New England and the upper Middle Atlantic. As a result, when the war started, the Union Army had few key army officers, but the Union Navy remained largely intact.

The Union used its naval superiority to effectively blockade Southern ports, leaving the South no way to export its cotton. The Confederates countered by trying to invent new devices to inflict "asymmetric warfare" on the Union Navy in the form of fast blockade runners and specialized, short-range armored ships for attacking Union naval vessels. In the South, however, the term "spy ship" amounted to taking row boats out of harbors at night to discover the Union ships' positions in hopes of helping any departing blockade runners. The Southerners might not have been high tech spies, but they obviously did not lack courage. If they accidentally rowed too close to a Union ship and were discovered, they did not return to shore.

The Union Navy also supported Grant's army in its remarkable campaign against Vicksburg on the Mississippi River. It assisted the capture of New Orleans by General Butler's forces, and it supported and eventually rescued McClellan's magnificent army in its absurd campaign on the southern Virginia peninsula. In addition, Union ships landed reconnaissance teams and spies outside the range of major fortresses on the Southern coast to support intelligence operations against the Confederacy. No specialized spy vessels were built for these missions. The Union Navy simply picked smaller ships with shallower drafts to enable the crews to approach the coast closely before depositing or recovering spies on shore.

The Union Navy operated abroad, as well, with intelligence missions in foreign ports to support efforts to sabotage any foreign aid to the Confederacy. In October of 1861, Union spies reported to the Union Navy that two Confederate "commissioners," John Slidell and James Mason, had landed in Havana, Cuba and were welcomed in the British Embassy there. The Union Navy correctly assumed that the two Confederate commissioners would sail to England aboard a British vessel, and that they would work to gain British support for the Confederacy when they arrived in England.

When Slidell and Mason went aboard the British merchant ship *Trent*, the Union sloop USS *San Jacinto* was waiting for them off of Havana. The *San Jacinto* fired across the bow of the *Trent*, and when the *Trent* came to, Union Marines boarded it and illegally removed Slidell and Mason by force to the *San Jacinto* against the loud protest of the *Trent's* British captain. The *San Jacinto* took the Confederate agents to the United States for incarceration. The mission was a huge momentary success for the Union and provided great entertainment for the sailors and Marines of the *San Jacinto*. It was also a prime example of the important difference between *acquiring* intelligence and *acting* on intelligence wisely.

Naturally, Confederate President Jefferson Davis and his chorus of professional complainers howled bitterly about the *Trent* incident. With cotton no longer exportable from the South, righteous indignation became the Confederacy's chief export product. Everyone outside of the Confederacy responded the way they usually did to Davis's near-daily righteous theatrics. They ignored him.

The United Kingdom also howled in protest, and Lincoln had to calm the many foolish politicians in Washington. Lincoln ignored the literary drama the Northern presses printed, apologized to the United Kingdom, and released the two Confederate agents. As Lincoln put it, "One war at a time, folks. One war at a time."

During the Civil War, every Union-controlled ship visiting any foreign port was prepared to retrieve information on land or to retrieve agents as circumstances dictated. The Union's naval intelligence operations had three important impacts on how the Union conducted the Civil War. First, they provided tactical intelligence about Confederate troop dispositions and conditions in the Confederate coastal areas. Second, they supplied Lincoln's administration with clear information about the United Kingdom's unwillingness to enter the war on the side of the Confederacy. And third, they helped keep Union armies operating in the Western theater, such as Mississippi, Arkansas, and Louisiana, informed of Confederate troop strengths and locations. Overall, the advantage of spy ships was critical in tipping the balance of the US Civil War in favor of the North.

5

SPY SHIPS IN WWI

AFTER THE CIVIL WAR, INTEREST IN FUNDING THE US NAVY declined, and the United States entered another period of isolation. Pacific region nations offered no significant naval competition, and European countries were continuing their long-standing tradition of alternately allying with and invading each other. Congress and the public felt no compelling need to construct a great US Navy and remained focused on continental expansion and westward migration across the continent. The central US military theme during this period was the Indian Wars carried out by the US Army at the expense of Native American tribes.

US spy ship activity continued at a minimal level with a focus on the Caribbean Sea and South America. European powers also maintained an interest in controlling South American nations, but Europe's internal conflicts prevented it from effectively exercising imperial interests in Central and South America. As a result, from the 1870s until 1898, the United States conducted no major naval intelligence efforts beyond the normal diplomacy and observations carried out by US Navy vessels on routine foreign port visits. In contrast, European navies were more active in intelligence and supported the continuing European conflicts with aggressive spy ship activities. The French and British navies, in particular, maintained organized naval intelligence efforts against each other.

During the late nineteenth century, Europe's single greatest potential impact on the Americas was the French effort to build a canal across Panama. At the time, the French were not our enemies, but many other European countries were. If the French had built and controlled a Panama canal, they would have determined who used that critical passage.

Europe was already expanding its naval influence in the Pacific, and with a canal, the French could have allowed a preponderance of enemy forces to move quickly to our Pacific coast in the event of a war, making our potential European enemies a bi-coastal issue. The French also could have prevented the United States from using the canal, giving European nations a decided advantage. Fortunately, the French were doomed to failure due to poor reconnaissance and planning. However, their efforts at building a canal in Panama served as a wakeup call to the United States and helped to convince the US taxpayers and Congress to fund modernization of the US Navy on a moderate scale.

After the assassination of President Garfield in 1881, Chester Arthur assumed the US presidency and brought two strong visions with him to the White House. His first vision was for the reform of the US government and the implementation of the civil service test system. His second great vision involved recognizing the importance of international affairs and foreign trade. Arthur was convinced that the safety of the United States depended in large part on the revitalization of the US Navy.

The American people agreed. The United States wasn't that far removed from the War of 1812, during which the British sailed up the Potomac and burned Washington, DC. European countries were in expansionist mode at that time, and France had even tried to invade Mexico. The only thing that protected the United States from rampant European imperialism was a big ocean, and we Americans wanted to keep that ocean as big as we could by investing in a better US Navy. As a result, Congress authorized the construction of a few modern, expensive steel ships.

As revolutionary activity in Spain's Caribbean and Philippine colonies increased (see *Key People & Wars*), the US Navy took a growing interest in gathering intelligence from both areas. In 1882, in response to its new emphasis on foreign trade and international diplomacy, the US government openly funded formal intelligence work by founding the first independent US intelligence service, the Office of Naval Intelligence ("ONI"). During the first twelve years of its history, the ONI remained aloof of Washington politics and was wildly successful in gathering intelligence in Asia and South America.

By 1893, the US Navy was using ONI as a tool for supporting its funding requests and strategic debates. In the years leading up to the Spanish American War, the ONI was somewhat distracted by the politics in Washington, but by returning to the Civil War tactics of using naval vessels for landing and retrieving agents at night, they provided critical intelligence from the Philippines, Puerto Rico, and Cuba. One of the most important pieces of information that the ONI delivered to the US government was an accurate assessment of Spain's large-but-declining navy.

Naval Intelligence accurately predicted that, due to a lack of adequate colliers for replenishing coal, Spain would limit its fleet operations to essential areas in the Caribbean and the Philippines and would not risk an escalation of the war by attacking US cities. By knowing this, the United States took advantage of Spain's economic problems and her inability to properly support long-range operations in distant waters by concentrating US naval forces on blockading Cuba and supporting amphibious operations in Cuba, Puerto Rico, and the Philippines. As a result, the United States wrestled Guam, Puerto Rico, and the Philippines away from Spain and established friendly relations and strong trade with a newly-independent Cuba.

That was to be the ONI's last significant achievement for years to come. Throughout history, politicians have succumbed to the temptation to turn intelligence communities into their personal cheerleading sections for their political agendas, and in the early twentieth century, US politicians proved they could succumb with the best of them. During that period, civilian political forces controlling the ONI exercised such a strong influence over intelligence officers that the ONI began to resemble a political propaganda agency rather than an independent intelligence service. It routinely subverted its own best officers in order to provide reports that were politically acceptable to the Secretary of the Navy, the White House, and Congress.

As Europe spiraled toward the tragedy of WWI, individual intelligence officers aboard US ships and working from US consulates and embassies often produced good work, but they were mostly ignored by the ONI leadership, which was mostly busy pumping out custom print jobs ordered up by politicians. A review of old intelligence reports submitted by US ships during this period reveals a lack of enthusiasm on the part of approximately one-third of the intelligence officers at sea. Reading the reports submitted by naval personnel at US consulates and embassies reveals a similar state of affairs. Inconvenient facts were nowhere welcome in Washington.

As WWI became inevitable, one of the new weapons available to US Naval Intelligence services was the submarine. In the absence of radar and sonar, which were both WWII developments, submarines presented a marvelous opportunity for conducting intelligence operations on enemy shores. However, they were not employed in this role by either the United Kingdom or the United States.

Also, the United States and the United Kingdom did not understand how the Germans would use submarines and surface commerce raiders, which are military ships that pursue merchant ships. It's not that individual intelligence officers couldn't imagine the possibilities. Individuals *did* predict the threat from the U-boats, but overall, the leadership at ONI didn't take them seriously. The occasional brilliant, accurate reports that young intelligence officers dared to submit on the threat of submarines were routinely discarded as a result of political pressure from Congress and the White House.

This was not solely a US problem, as the United Kingdom had its head shoved into the same U-boats-aren't-so-bad sandbank. Even the highly-respected British Admiral of the Fleet 1st Earl John Jellicoe was ignored when he recommended convoying. He warned that the United Kingdom could lose the war at sea without ever fighting a major engagement if German submarines were not stopped from sinking British and allied shipping. It did not fit the narrative of the day, which was that the U-boats weren't that much of a threat, and that convoying would not make the merchant ships that much safer.

It's easy to look back now at the devastation wrought by the German U-boats and shake our heads at how the ONI leadership and politicians could have missed such an obvious threat. Why didn't shipping merchants form convoys escorted by the Navy or the Coast Guard at the first sign of danger?

In our opinion, one major reason was because the threat from the U-boats was a financially inconvenient truth. Many politicians, military officers, and shipping magnates were averse to the idea of convoys, as they were expensive for both the military and for shipping companies. That's because to convoy effectively, the companies had to place their shipping schedules under the control of the Navy. That means that ships might have sat loaded in port and ready to depart for an undetermined period while enough ships prepare to convoy, and that was a costly proposition. As for the Navy, it would have had to devote resources to protecting the convoys of merchant ships, which was also an expensive proposition in ships and manpower.

Another reason the United States and the United Kingdom did not immediately enact convoys in response to the German U-boat threat was that many in politics, shipping, and the military were unconvinced that convoys were safer for the ships. Support for convoys was not universal within any faction of the US or UK governments, and many merchantmen believed the convoys would draw more fire than a sole ship anyway. The shipping companies considered the loss of a couple ships now and then to be merely the cost of doing business, and it was an uphill battle to convince them of the safety of convoys, even though statistics and historical analysis made it clear that chances of survival were much higher in escorted groups.

Also, the United States and the United Kingdom focused on winning major naval engagements between capital ships, which are battleships and heavy cruisers. Locked into that mindset, they could not see and understand the threat posed by small "asymmetrical" weapons and tactics such as the German U-boat. Therefore, many believed the US Navy was exaggerating the risks.

Again, it's easy to look back and criticize, but we need look no further than cyberattacks to see a contemporary comparison to that "see no evil" state of mind regarding the German U-boats. Regardless of warnings from tech-savvy military and intelligence personnel, politicos and members of Congress hire unscreened foreign nationals from hostile nations for their Information Technology services, and they continue to use unsecured phones, computers, and servers. Even after such behavior on the part of those in government has compromised top secret programs, resulted in hacks of Pentagon databases, and gotten hundreds of our own people killed, it's a real fight for the Intelligence Community to get people in the government to take cyberthreats seriously. It is too convenient for people to pretend they are alone in their room with their Android, Galaxy, Blackberry, laptop, Smart TV, Alexa, etc. No doubt some historians will look back and shake their heads, just as we are tempted to do with the German U-boat threat of the early twentieth century.

The Office of Naval Intelligence's overall failure to predict the risks the German submarines and surface raiders posed to the economy of the United Kingdom in its official reports was one of the ONI's greatest intelligence failures leading up to WWI. The United States, France, and the United Kingdom could have dealt with the U-boats if they were willing to step up to the task. In the two decades leading up to WWI, both the United States and the United Kingdom had the ships and personnel necessary to conduct effective ship-based spying on Germany, but they lacked the administrative freedom to use the intelligence gained to provide meaningful independent reports.

As a result of this underestimation of the enemy, the Germans were wildly successful at interdicting commerce between the Allied nations in the Atlantic and the Mediterranean. In March of 1917 alone, the Germans sank 25 percent of the merchant ships bound for the United Kingdom, reducing Britain's grain reserves to a mere six-week supply.

When the US joined the war in April of 1917, the British Admiralty had sporadic convoys for troop ships and some food ships from The Netherlands. US Navy Adm. W. S. Sims set out to convince the British War Cabinet to start routine convoys for all merchant ships. The British government agreed to try one. The first British merchant convoy sailed from the United Kingdom in May 1917 and arrived in Gibraltar intact. The Admiralty then ordered that all ships bound for Britain should be escorted in convoys.

The British requested US ships to assist with this effort. The United States responded and established "Base No. 9" at Gibraltar on July 5, 1917. Six US Coast Guard Cutters and thirty-five US Navy vessels were sent to Base 9 during the course of WWI, where they escorted 10,478 voyages. It is worth noting that the US Coast Guard's primary duty during WWI was to escort convoys in the Atlantic and from Base 9 in Gibraltar. As a result of battles with the German U-boats and commerce raiders, the US Coast Guard suffered the highest casualty rate of all US military branches in the course of the war.

The spy ships were available, but the US and UK governments wanted their intelligence communities to provide assessments that best matched their impressions and agendas rather than assessments that matched the facts. It was a mistake that would be repeated only three decades later in WWII and frequently since then. This failure illustrates of one of the most important intelligence questions that can never be answered by intelligence services in any democratic society: How can a nation ensure that intelligence gathered by its services will be recognized, understood, and responded to by the decision makers beyond the intelligence services? We do not yet know the answer.

6

SPY SHIPS AND THE PATH TO WWII

AT THE CONCLUSION OF WWI, SOME PARTICIPANT COUNTRIES WERE convinced that the world was now safe for democracy, and they drastically reduced their military budgets in an attempt to develop viable national economies. Germany, on the other hand, was convinced there would be another war, and that Germany would be victorious and vindicate itself from the defeat it suffered. Japan was also convinced that large-scale war would continue, and that Japan would continue to profit by war as it had done in WWI and during earlier wars with Russia, Korea, and China. As for Russia, it was in the middle of a communist revolution that both surprised and frightened many Western governments. In the political climate of the times, spy ships of one type or another were a natural occurrence.

One of the most interesting spy ship operations of the Post-WWI Era was carried out by the Royal Navy against the Soviet Union from small bases in Finland. The United Kingdom supported the White Russian faction against the Communist faction, but that support was limited by political realities at home. At that time, the UK taxpayers, potential draftees, and their loved ones were certain that war could and should be avoided at nearly any cost. Also, the United Kingdom was having difficulty acquiring intelligence from inside Russia. However, the Royal Navy scraped together effective operations against the Soviet Union with limited funds and even less political capital.

In that difficult political environment, the Royal Navy, with only a handful of people, set up a clandestine torpedo-boat base in Finland. With that base, the United Kingdom kept the Saint Petersburg port and the large Russian Baltic Fleet under effective surveillance by using the torpedo boats at night to transport agents into the Soviet Union through the heavily-defended Saint Petersburg sea island fortress network.

The United Kingdom also used the torpedo boats to extract agents from the Soviet Union who had been working for the British, but that proved to be more complicated. For one thing, extractions often took place because covers had been blown, so the agent being extracted was already being hunted. The Soviets were even more alert than usual if they knew there were agents on the run, so often, instead of using the torpedo boats, the British attempted to move the agents overland through Eastern Europe, Central Asia, or the Russian Far East.

The torpedo boats dropped off agents on the Russian Baltic Coast, reconnoitered, and snuck around conducting other espionage against the Leninists in the area. The Royal Navy had not envisioned that the small boats would be able to conduct raids against a war ship or a fortress with cannons. Then, on August 17–18, 1919, Royal Navy Commander (later Admiral) Claude Dobson said, "Hold my toddy," and his daring torpedo boat teams broke through to a new dimension of possibilities.

Late on the night of the seventeenth, Comdr. Dobson and approximately forty-six men in eight fifty-five foot torpedo boats sallied forth from their base in Finland in the Björkö Sound.

They ran the gauntlet of Soviet sea island fortresses, and seven of the boats slipped into the inner harbor of the Kronstadt Naval Base on Kotlin Island at the mouth of the St. Petersburg harbor. The eighth boat remained at the entrance of the harbor to cover their retreat.

The Brits attacked. In spite of being under fire from a Russian destroyer that was on patrol in the harbor, their torpedoes sank the six-thousand-ton cruiser *Pamiat Azova* and seriously damaged the seventeen-thousand-ton heavy cruiser *Andrei Pervozvanny* and the twenty-four-thousand-ton dreadnought *Petropavlovsk*. The British lost three boats, and they were not able to hit the destroyer. Eight men were killed, and nine men were captured. The surviving men and five boats made it out of the harbor and back to Finland.

Comdr. Dobson and Lt. Gordon Steele each received the Victoria Cross. The raid had been outrageous and daring, but such daring was not unusual for the Brits of the post-WWI era, and it was in the best tradition of great naval officer and semi-pirate Francis Drake. Comdr. Dobson and his men demonstrated that even small spy ships could do substantial damage to an enemy with active offensives.

In 1930, in an economic attempt to prevent another world war, France, Italy, Japan, the United Kingdom, and the United States signed the London Naval Treaty. The treaty limited the number and tonnage of large war ships and the use of submarines. Because Germany was already severely limited in naval construction by the Treaty of Versailles, it was not invited to join the treaty. The Soviet Union declined.

The London Naval Treaty was a reasonable attempt at avoiding an expensive and dangerous naval arms race, but it could only be effective if all of the signers followed the terms of the treaty, and if they could all be sure that they were all adhering to its terms.

France, Germany, the United Kingdom, and the United States all had merchant ships entering each other's harbors regularly and could easily observe any construction of large ships in each other's ports. Japan, on the other hand, had closed off foreign traffic from its home waters and the waters of its ex-German possessions in the Pacific. This meant that normal spy ship operations conducted by intelligence operatives could not be employed against Japan. By the time Japan signed the treaty in 1930, it already had plans to violate the agreement and did so without hesitation. These violations were later confirmed by professional baseball player and American intelligence operative Moe Berg during a team trip to Japan. (See *Key Figures in Espionage.*)

Nazi Germany did not foresee any significant operations in the Pacific and was not greatly concerned with Japan's naval construction, but France, The Netherlands, and the United Kingdom still had major colonial presences in the region and needed to gather intelligence concerning the growing Japanese military. As a Pacific nation, the United States had a strong interest in acquiring intelligence on the Japanese military, as well, but it was also barred from major Japanese ports.

Necessity being the mother of invention, and espionage being the child of necessity, all of the above nations, including Japan, resorted to new naval intelligence methods. They, along with other nations such as The Netherlands, developed the practice of hiring merchant seamen from any country that had trade access with any target nation. In some cases, trained intelligence officers were able to gain employment on merchant ships with useful shipping schedules and routes. In other cases, countries made efforts to recruit legitimate merchant seamen to moonlight as spies. In effect, each nation's own ships became spy ships being used against themselves.

Some of the more ambitious merchant sailors were even collecting salaries from four or five governments simultaneously, and they reported whatever fanciful stories they thought their benefactors might enjoy hearing. The Japanese used this "reverse spy ship" technique to great effect, and along with their land-based spies in the Philippines, Hawaii, and Singapore, they were able to accurately map the defenses of Manila Harbor, Pearl Harbor, and Singapore in preparation for attacks in December of 1941.

7

COLD WAR SPY SHIPS

THIS MAY SURPRISE READERS, BUT DURING WWII, SPY SHIPS WERE somewhat less useful. Ships couldn't quietly mosey past countries in international waters and expect those countries not to notice and capture or sink them. Submarine crews would attempt to glean whatever information they could; however, the electronics equipment on the submarines was far more limited than that on spy ships of the same era.

None of these factors kept the Soviets from attempting to use spy ships to surveil the United States, Canada, and the United Kingdom during WWII. While those three allied countries took great risks to send food and materials to the Soviet Union to keep it in the war against Germany, the Soviet Union used its merchant ships to spy on the United States and Canada and to deliver oil to Japan. To a degree, this assisted Japan in its war against the United States.

So why did the United States put up with that kind of double dealing on the part of the Soviet Union?

While all of this ring-around-the-rosy was happening with the Soviet Union in the Pacific, the Soviets were sending millions of their sons and daughters to the Eastern Front to fight the Germans, and it was in the US interests that the Soviets continue to make that immense sacrifice in human lives. Fortunately for us and unfortunately for the Russian people, Stalin was perfectly willing to sacrifice those sons and daughters. It saved him the expense of killing them all himself.

After WWII, spy ship activity by the United States and the Soviet Union grew by at least a factor of twenty and incorporated rapidly-changing technologies. Along with the United States and the Soviet Union, numerous countries in Europe, South America, Central America, Asia, and Africa used maritime platforms to varying degrees for intelligence-gathering operations. A nation's degree of participation in spy ship activities was, for the most part, determined by financial considerations rather than ethical or philosophical concerns.

As a result, the United States and the Soviet Union remained the pre-eminent players in seaborne intelligence activities, as well as in other types of intelligence. Both nations had large economies, and in an age when nuclear weapons and missiles to deliver them were becoming more deadly every year, both countries had massive amounts of money to spend pursuing their respective intelligence goals. In terms of both expense and manpower, both countries made a commitment to spy ships on a whole new scale, involving thousands of people and many millions of dollars.

The United States converted surplus WWII freighters to spy ship duty and built specially-equipped ships "from the keel up." Meanwhile, the Soviets took a less expensive approach. Though the Soviet Union built and manned a fleet of dozens of spy ships for operations against Western nations as well as against Japan, Taiwan, Malaysia, Indonesia, and South Africa (see Chapter

Eight), we could assume that nearly every Soviet ship that left Soviet waters was a spy ship. The Soviet intelligence services even expected real fishing vessels to remain observant and report all activity by any Western ships. In some cases, the Soviets furnished legitimate freighters with extra radio receivers, sonar equipment, radar detection equipment, recording equipment, and a few specialists to operate them as they made their voyages around the world. As a result, most of the Soviet Union's sea-based spying was done with fishing trawler hulls provided with adequate generators to run modest suites of electronics intelligence gear.

The US military and intelligence services referred to these trawlers as AGIs, which stood for Auxiliary General Intelligence. The trawlers' basic task was to patrol near the US coast, as well as near US foreign ports and other foreign naval bases. The Soviets collected intelligence via their various radio receivers, sonar sets, and radar detection equipment. In addition, they reported any visual observations of US naval activity to their headquarters. Besides operating near bases and ports, trawlers were tasked with trailing US Navy task forces and carrier groups at sea.

On several occasions, the modified Soviet fishing trawlers that prowled the US coasts ended up impounded at US Coast Guard bases on the Atlantic or Pacific coasts or in Guam. Those Soviet spy ship crews had several advantages over US spy ship crews. For one thing, the Soviets were always confident that US Navy and Coast Guard vessels would act reasonably and consistently. Even when they were impounded to US bases, the Soviet crews had no reason to fear torture or abuse, and in many instances, the greatest headache involved in capturing Soviet trawlers was convincing the Soviet crews to return to the Soviet Union.

In the 1950s, Soviet trawlers operating near the US coast intentionally damaged several trans-Pacific undersea communications cables. In one instance in February of 1959, twelve breaks occurred in five US transatlantic communications cables. The USS *Roy O. Hale* (DE-336) destroyer escort caught the Soviet trawler *Novorossiysk* off the coast of New England in the North Atlantic. The US Navy's boarding party accessed the trawler's log, and the log indicated quite clearly that the trawler had been present at the locations of the cable breaks at the time the cables were broken. Furthermore, the Americans found pieces of American cable that were still on the trawler.

Holmes has the impression that the Soviet sailors didn't think the destroyer escort would actually board them so they didn't bother hiding or destroying the evidence. The Soviets claimed it was an unjustified boarding, but the United States pointed out that under the terms of the Convention for the Protection of Submarine Telegraph Cables of 1884, which Russia had signed, the United States had the right to board that trawler. The United States filed diplomatic protests with the Soviet Union Ministry of Foreign Affairs and was met with the standard Soviet denials.

A glance at the seemingly decrepit trawlers might lead one to assume that "bottom of the barrel" members of the Soviet Navy manned them. However, their crews were well-trained Soviet Navy personnel who the Komitet Gosudarstvennoy Bezopasnosti ("KGB") had carefully screened for defection risk. When the fast-maneuvering ships of the US Coast Guard, such as the Hamilton class Cutters, impounded Soviet trawlers, defections did, in fact, occur; however, the US Coast Guard had instructions to minimize and discourage defections by the Soviet crews.

When Soviet sailors did manage to defect, the United States did everything in its power to keep the defections quiet to avoid a propaganda counterattack by the Soviet Union. Given that the defection of Soviet sailors from captured spy ships left the United States open to charges of kidnapping, the White House and the State Department preferred defections to take place under less ambiguous circumstances.

Besides gathering intelligence, the Soviet trawlers sometimes engaged in harassment operations. The trawler crews made two assumptions. One was that the US Navy and her allies would exercise restraint when responding to trawlers. The other was that skilled US and NATO professionals would avoid mishaps with recklessly-piloted Soviet vessels. By 1960, the Soviet trawler crews were growing bolder in their approaches to US naval vessels. When US carrier planes practiced bombing runs against the wakes of their carriers with unarmed practice bombs, the trawlers maneuvered into the carrier wake close to the US ships and interfered with those practices.

In another harassing tactic, trawlers positioned themselves ahead of US Navy vessels and then turned in front of those vessels' hulls. Clearly, the Soviet crews had both courage and plenty of faith that their opponents would exercise great restraint. In particular, when US and Allied ships were refueling while underway at sea, trawlers caused tremendous consternation by maneuvering into the paths of the ships and the oilers tethered to them. Frequently, Soviet trawlers delayed fueling operations until US destroyers forced them away from the fueling ships.

A third important task for the trawlers was to spy on any Western missile tests conducted at sea from civilian test ships, submarines, or other naval vessels. These test range spy operations yielded tremendous results for the Soviets and were well worth the effort and minor expense that they invested.

After the Cuban Missile Crisis of 1962, the White House authorized the Pentagon to take a more aggressive posture toward trawlers that endangered US vessels or directly hampered opera-

tions in international waters. The Pentagon set strict rules about
how far Navy ships could go in responding to harassing trawlers.
The US vessels were permitted to closely approach the trawlers
and even bump them if necessary. They were also permitted,
when possible, to foul the trawlers' propulsion screws with cables
to disable them, but they were not permitted to sink the trawlers.

The Soviet trawlers were not as easy to harass as desk-bound officers in the Pentagon assumed. On paper it all seemed simple
enough, but at sea, it was not quite so easy. The trawlers were
slower than US Navy ships, but they were highly maneuverable,
and bumping them with just the right amount of speed was a
tricky proposition. As any two ships approach on a near-parallel
course at even a moderate speed, a pressure wave builds up
between the two ships, and the pressure varies as the distance of
the two vessels changes. This makes bumping quite tricky.

When US destroyers attempted bumps, the Soviet crews were
usually able to turn away just in time to avoid them. Naturally,
these same destroyers were often equipped with extra electronics
equipment and personnel. It is a testament to the skill of both the
Soviet and Allied sailors during the Cold War that, in spite of the
thousands of close contacts between US carrier group vessels and
Soviet trawlers, there were no serious collisions.

In 1965, the United States commissioned a new class of spy ship,
the Banner class ships,, which it intended to use to approach
Soviet waters more closely. Small by US standards, they were 176
feet in length and more maneuverable than other US Navy spy
ships then in operation.

In June of 1966, the USS *Banner* entered contested waters when
she crossed the entrance to the Bay of Cape Povorotny. The
Soviets responded by dispatching a squadron of destroyers and
several patrol craft to harass the *Banner*. The incident ended with
a collision between the *Banner* and the Soviet trawler *Anemometr*.

No serious injuries were reported, and both sides chose to keep the incident quiet. However, the intelligence gathered by the USS *Banner* during this and similar operations was considered to be of extremely high value by both the US Navy and the US Intelligence Community in general.

With the Vietnam conflict in the 1960s came an increased presence of both US warships and Soviet vessels in the Gulf of Tonkin, and more dangerous incidents occurred. On two occasions, Soviet and US ships made sufficiently hard contact to cause moderate damage. In the Sea of Japan, closer to their home ports and Soviet air bases, the Soviet trawlers tended to be even more aggressive with US ships. As a result, in 1967, after much nagging by the Pentagon, the US State Department delivered proposed Rules of Engagement for contacts between Soviet and US vessels at sea.

The Soviets initially ignored the proposal, but by the late 1960s, the Soviet Defense Ministry and Soviet Navy were finally developing and operating credible war ships in the Mediterranean and other international waters, and those assets were not as disposable as the trawlers had been. The harassment game became more balanced, and the Soviets had more reason to avoid collisions at sea.

In 1971, talks concerning rules for contact between the United States and the Soviet Union began in earnest. By that time, the Soviet Navy was actually impatient to conclude an agreement. They had decided to captain and man their newer, larger deep sea naval vessels with young personnel, who had more modern training, rather than their older senior officers and senior petty officers. In the long run, this provided the best results for the Soviets, but in the short term with so many inexperienced personnel at sea, they were concerned that their youngsters would miscalculate and cause a serious incident that could result in a political defeat for the Soviet Navy at the Politburo, along with a reduction in the Navy's already sparse funding. Denting or sinking a cheap trawler was one thing. Damaging an expensive new Soviet destroyer or cruiser would be quite another.

In Moscow on May 25, 1972, while the Cold War was raging, the Soviet Union and the United States quietly signed an agreement that both sides could live with. Although the agreement did not completely eliminate incidents at sea between the two nations, it greatly reduced them. The trawlers continued their spy work, but usually with more cautious behavior, and Soviet submarines increasingly joined the boats in their spy efforts. Even today, forty-something years later, Russian trawlers remain an inexpensive and highly-effective intelligence platform for the former Soviet Union.

Around October of 1971, the US Navy Office of Naval Intelligence ("ONI"), in conjunction with the National Security Agency ("NSA") executed Operation Ivy Bells, a joint espionage venture with the purpose of collecting Soviet communications. The USS *Halibut* nuclear submarine traveled to the Sea of Okhotsk, and, using a somewhat experimental divers' lockout system, US Navy divers located the four-hundred-foot-deep Soviet naval communications cable. The divers installed a twenty-foot-long apparatus that wrapped around the Soviet cable without piercing or damaging the cable system. It was also designed to automatically detach if the Soviets should bring the cable up.

A recording device was connected to the apparatus, and it collected all of the Soviet communications that passed through the cable. Each month, US Navy divers went back in the water to collect the recordings and install new tapes. The collected recordings were then turned over to the NSA, and much of the information gleaned was shared with the CIA. The United States realized as early as the first tapes that the Soviets were confident of their cable system, and that most of their transmissions were unencrypted. Those transmissions gave the United States a comprehensive intelligence picture of the operations that were going on at Russia's nearby Petropavlovsk Naval Base in Northeast Russia.

Most of the sailors on board the USS *Halibut* did not know the nature of Operation Ivy Bells, and they thought they were in the area trying to recover missile parts from a Soviet missile test. Although it was a cover story, the divers actually did recover debris from a Soviet SS-N-12 anti-ship missile, so it was an added bonus to the mission. In fact, the recovered debris turned out to be its own coup, as the United States was able to gather enough information from it to quickly develop effective countermeasures. All in all, a good month for the US Navy.

The NSA did excellent work on Operation Ivy Bells, but there was a traitor in their midst. An NSA agent named Ronald Pelton was dissatisfied with his position, and he quit the agency in a fit of anger. Pelton was in deep debt and had personal finance management issues. Three months after walking off the job, he filed for bankruptcy. Then, in January of 1980, Pelton walked into the Soviet Embassy in DC and offered to sell the KGB what he knew.

Pelton sang to the KGB for three years, from 1980 through 1983, and he only received $35k for his gold mine of sensitive information. He sold the information on Operation Ivy Bells for a measly $5k. In other words, Pelton wasn't just a dirtbag traitor, he sold cheaper than a five dollar hooker on discount day. The Soviets didn't act immediately on the information, presumably to give them time to sow disinformation.

Then, in July of 1985, KGB Colonel Vitaly Yurchenko gave us the information that led to the arrest of Ronald Pelton. Yurchenko also gave us the information that should have led to the arrest of Edward Lee Howard, but Howard evaded surveillance with the help of a blow up sex doll* and escaped to the Soviet Union—a story for another day. Pelton was convicted of espionage crimes in 1986, and he spent almost thirty years in prison before his release on November 24, 2015, at the age of seventy-four. By our estimation, his release was approximately fifty years too early.

Although the Soviet trawlers were part of a system that Holmes has spent his life opposing in one form or another, we must grant some respect, if not appreciation, for the efforts of the Soviet trawler crews. They went to sea for long cruises—often six months—in uncomfortable vessels that were more like over-sized toys. The Soviet crews turned those little trawlers across the paths of oncoming US ships, even aircraft carriers, risking being sunk by any US ship that might have miscalculated their relative positions and speeds.

Though that degree of recklessness was dialed back for some time, Russian trawlers and freighters are once again becoming more aggressive in their risks. It seems that Czar Putin is more willing than the old Soviets to escalate a conflict between Russia and the US Navy. We shall see where that takes us.

*While younger operatives and officers will say blow up sex dolls were never used, and that the Intelligence Community always used some form of pop up doll instead, Holmes clearly remembers otherwise. He still laughs about all those straight-laced young office types being sent out to the sex shops in the area to purchase blow up sex dolls for the science types to modify for operations.

8

SOVIET AND RUSSIAN SPY SHIPS

FROM THE 1970S UNTIL THE COLLAPSE OF THE SOVIET UNION IN 1991, the Soviets continued to invest heavily in their spy ship programs. Even their smallest and most dilapidated trawlers were equipped with decent electronics equipment and top notch sailors and technicians. The officers were rotated from among the ranks of experienced combat ship officers, and they and all of their crew members underwent re-vetting and screening by the KGB staff to assure their political loyalty.

In the 1970s, the Soviet government finally decided to fund a purpose-built intelligence ship for the Soviet Navy. Their first class of purpose-built intelligence ships was designated as "Project 1826" by the Soviets and the "Balzam" class by NATO. These ships displaced 4900 tons of water and were a major upgrade from Soviet ad hoc auxiliaries like the trawlers in both capability and living conditions for their crews. In addition to a complete suite of receiver antennas and active radar, they were built with both hull-mounted sonar and variable depth towed array sonar for tracking submarines. They were also equipped with basic anti-aircraft missiles and a 30 mm close-in weapons system for defense against anti-ship missiles. The disadvantage of arming these ships with visible mounted weapons systems was that the Soviet Union could no longer claim that they were unarmed research vessels.

Four Balzam class ships were commissioned into the Soviet Navy between 1980 and 1987, and one of them, the *Belomore*, remains in service today with the Russian Northern Fleet. The Soviets intended to use these ships to monitor testing of the US Navy's rapid technological evolution in ships and weapons that was accelerating during the 1970s and 1980s.

In 1980, the Soviet government approved a more expensive and capable class of spy ships designated "Project 864" by the Soviets and the "Meridian" class by NATO. These ships are slightly lighter than the preceding Balzam class ships, but they are significantly improved in their electronics equipment, their sonar arrays, and their more powerful and efficient satellite communications equipment. The newer communications equipment allowed for rapid and reliable transfer of collected data to shore stations in the Soviet Union. The Meridians' weaponry was also upgraded with the addition of a second 30MM close-in weapons system and a better weapons control system. Seven Meridian class ships were commissioned by the Soviets between 1985 and 1988, and all seven of them remain in commission in the Russian Navy.

Since the fall of the Soviet Union in 1991, various Russian Navy shipbuilding projects have been reduced or completely cancelled. Many Russian Navy submarines and ships have been sold off or scrapped in order to reduce maintenance and operations costs. The fact that all seven of the Meridian class intelligence ships have remained in operation without suffering from a reduction in maintenance or manpower should tell us how high of a priority the Russian government has consistently placed on spying on the US Navy.

Holmes and many others take it as an indication that while the Cold War might have ended for the United States, it never ended for the Russian military oligarchy and Russian intelligence services. Russian spy ships have continued to operate in international waters in close proximity to US Navy bases, to other NATO member navy bases, and to US and various NATO at-sea weapons and systems tests and war game exercises.

Occasionally, such as in December of 2019, we see media reports of a Russian spy ship off the US coast. The story is generally presented as a shocking new revelation. It is only shocking to those journalists who have no basic knowledge of the twenty-first century operations of the Russian Navy.

Every year since the fall of the Soviet Empire in 1991, the Russians have operated spy ships in international waters close to the US coast and the UK coast. Before that, the Soviets operated spy ships in international waters near the US coast and the UK coast every year since 1945. On occasion, when Soviet spy ships strayed within US territorial waters, they were either boarded and inspected or captured and impounded by the US Navy and US Coast Guard. Since the fall of the Soviet Union, Russia has been more careful about not entering US territorial waters with their spy ships, and the United States has not impounded any Russian ships.

The other periodic Russian Navy activity that gets our attention is when one of the Russian Navy's ships bumps or comes danger-ously close to US Navy warships, as happened in January of 2020. These incidents of direct-but-moderate aggression by the Russian Navy might seem irrational at first glance. They are not going to cause the US Navy to modify its strategies or operations, so what is the value of the risky bumping incidents?

We should consider two factors. The first factor is that the Russians always use a relatively cheap, sturdy, low tech ship to cut off or bump a very expensive and high tech US Navy ship. That way, the Russians have less at risk in the incident than the United States does. The second thing to consider is that funding for the Russian Navy is always in tight competition with the Russian intelligence services, the Russian Air Force, the Russian Army, the Russian Missile Forces, and the Russian Space Forces for dwindling financial resources, and the bumping gives the Russian Navy the appearance of doing something important.

Vladimir Putin has always presented a platform of "returning Russia to her glory days of [a largely imagined] superpower domination over the world." While the bumping incidents might seem childish and useless to us, to Putin and his government, they seem like small victories over the still-evil United States. Amidst frequent equipment failures, serious accidents, and an ongoing low rate of operational availability of Russian Navy ships, they give the Russian Navy a chance to claim some relevance. This reinforces the Russian Navy's claims of being worthy of more funding.

To understand Russian spy ship and Russian naval activity in general in the post-Cold War era, we must try to imagine the primitive world view and the urgent propaganda needs of Vladimir Putin. For Putin, visibly operating spy ships against the United States is far more important than whatever intelligence those ships might gather. As a result, approximately 70 percent of Russia's naval operations are now all about being seen for the foreign and domestic propaganda value in an attempt to convince the rest of the world that the Russian Navy is still powerful.

Without the impression that Big Daddy Vlady is busy fending off mostly-imaginary, but exceedingly dangerous US aggression, the Russian people have one less reason to tolerate him.

For more on Vladimir Putin, see Chapter Twenty-nine.

9

CHINESE SPY SHIPS

In contrast to Russia, the navy of the People's Republic of China is not weak, nor does it care to be visible. The People's Liberation Army Navy, a.k.a. the Chinese Navy, is expanding and improving rapidly, and it has vast spy ship capabilities that it uses as clandestinely as possible.

To understand the spy ships of the PRC, it's worth considering China's strategic maritime priorities. There are several factors driving the PRC's maritime strategies—about 1.4 billion of them. That number increases daily. China's massive population greatly influences every aspect of its modern life and communist governments policies, including its navy.

As early as 700 BC, when most governments could not yet contemplate anything as complicated as a small bridge project, Han Chinese governments were constructing massive defensive wall systems. Large populations, relative to the period, allowed for large ideas. By comparison, today in the United States, some people can't conceive of projects on the scale of a basic border wall between the United States and Mexico. In some other nations, the idea of a building a fresh water system for its citizens involves a scale of work not yet acceptable in their culture.

Not so in China.

Thinking big is an ancient Han Chinese habit. An individual member of modern Chinese society is used to accepting tight limitations on their own personal aspirations, but they comfortably accept, and even expect, grand scale changes for their society.

The PRC's ambitious maritime priorities are driven by both domestic economic considerations and imperial aspirations. As communists, the Chinese would be aghast at the suggestion that they would be capable of imperialist ideas. The reality is that the Chinese are and have been capable of imperial aspirations since about 1000 BC. They were Chinese long before they were communists, and when you've had three thousand years of empire building, you develop great skills for pretending that you are not imperialist.

Such debates about whether or not the Chinese are imperialistic are more philosophical and comical in nature than they are practical. For our purposes, we will consider the Chinese maritime outlook and its spy ship efforts and leave it up to the individual reader to decide the right name for Communist China's strategies and aspirations.

As recently as the 1970s, Chinese spy ship efforts centered on three basic methods. The first basic method relied on Chinese cargo ships. All Chinese cargo ships were responsible for gathering naval and maritime intelligence as they travelled the world. The second, more local method, relied on Chinese fishing vessels. All Chinese fishing vessels, large and small, were required to report on anything that they saw or imagined that they saw. To manage these two low tech, high labor maritime intelligence efforts, the Chinese had to develop a huge bureaucracy.

The Communist government founded that bureaucracy, the Chinese Maritime Militia ("CMM"), in 1927 and has expanded and perfected it continuously to this day since its inception. Thanks to the CMM, China has been able to remain well-informed on maritime matters in the West Pacific region since 1927.

As the PRC's ship numbers have grown, so has its Maritime Militia. By 1970, the CMM had increased in organization, training, and communications ability and expanded its responsibilities beyond intelligence gathering to act as an auxiliary to the Chinese Coast Guard and Chinese Navy for law enforcement, resource hording, and the intimidation of neighboring states.

The PRC's third method of gathering maritime intelligence more closely matches the methods employed by the United States and its Western and Asian allies. Every Chinese naval vessel acts as a spy ship.

Thanks to the insane nature of dictator Mao Zedong's ruthless policies, the PRC's cargo fleet remained small and dilapidated. Killing tens of millions of its own citizens while attempting to completely control the lives of all the survivors required enormous allocations of manpower and material. As a result, even with generous technical assistance from Russia, the PRC was not able to build an effective navy during the reign of Chairman Mao. In 1976, Mao committed his first effective act as the leader of China. He died.

The oligarchy that replaced Mao was determined to engage the outside world in commerce and effective diplomacy. They were also determined to overcome the disastrous policies that Mao had instituted. While continuing to preach about the moral superiority of communist economics, they undertook the monumental task of pivoting toward a highly-regulated, but predominantly capitalist, economic system. The imagined shift in economic and foreign policies was no less breathtaking in scale than the decision to build of the Great Wall of China, and like the Great Wall, it didn't happen overnight. Nevertheless, in its authoritarian manner, China got it done.

This vast shift has had many side effects in Chinese society. Infant mortality fell and large-scale executions ceased. At the same time, the PRC became more urban and, perhaps, more urbane. These changes led to consumerism on a Western scale.

Consumerism, modernization, and a higher standard of living pushed up Chinese consumption of coal, oil, natural gas, other minerals, and all types of food. When 1.4 billion people need their dinner, the country needs vast amounts of food. This drove two important dynamics in the PRC's government planning, foreign policy, and military strategy.

First, the ability to import petroleum from the world's major petroleum producers has become a matter of survival for the PRC. A barrel of oil from Iran must travel through the tumultuous and unstable Persian Gulf area, then past China's archenemy India, through the Malacca Strait at Singapore, through Malaysian and Indonesian territorial waters, and finally through the waters of Vietnam to reach the nearest Chinese ports. In 2019, approximately 69 percent of China's petroleum was imported. China is very aware of its vulnerability in oil.

At the same time, China increasingly coveted mineral and fishing resources in the East and South China Seas and beyond. Vietnam, Malaysia, Indonesia, Brunei, the Philippines, Taiwan, South

Korea, and Japan also find those resources attractive. All of those factors have driven the PRC's willingness to invest heavily in maritime intelligence.

In 1991, as the Soviet Union collapsed and Russia's spy ship efforts temporarily slowed, China increased its efforts in maritime intelligence and naval construction. Now in 2020, as Russia operates all of eight purpose-built spy ships and three special-purpose submarines for mapping, tapping, and, if needed, cutting marine cables, China operates fifty-one purpose-built spy ships.

The Chinese Navy's current inventory of ships includes fourteen different specialized designs for everything from missile tracking, oceanographic mapping, and signals intelligence. Until 2019, China enjoyed an increasing budget and was willing to constantly upgrade its spy ship designs as they were produced. Now, around half of the Chinese Navy's spy ships are high quality, with excellent signals intelligence and analysis abilities.

In addition to the Chinese Navy's excellent spy ship program, the CMM has greatly improved its electronics equipment over the last two decades. While most CMM ships are less well-equipped for sophisticated signals intelligence missions than the Chinese Navy spy ships, the Chinese have brought them to a high standard in communications and networking equipment, and their shore-based command and control centers are well-manned and well-equipped. To Holmes's knowledge, the only estimate of the size of the CMM was released by China in 1978. At the time, China claimed 750,000 members, employing 180,000 ships.

To understand this claim, we have to understand that nearly any Chinese civilian vessel that can go to sea is incorporated into the CMM. The sailors might fish in earnest or haul cargo to Hong Kong, but they are also militia members. The number of vessels in the CMM has likely not grown much since 1978, but the average size of those vessels *has* grown. In many cases, their level of armaments has increased, and their electronics equipment has vastly improved. The sheer size of the CMM means that China is well-informed about all maritime and coastal activities in the Western Pacific region.

The obvious question is what does the People's Republic of China intend to do with these vast maritime and naval resources? Many Westerners understand that China wants to control the Pacific Ocean from the western coast of Korea to the southern tip of Japan, to the west coast of the Philippines, to the north shores of Indonesia and Malaysia, and to the east coast of Vietnam. This much China openly admits and, in fact, loudly proclaims. China has attempted to bolster these claims by manufacturing artificial islands on various reefs across that vast region. Along with all of China's maritime neighbors, international courts and the United Nations ("UN") flatly reject these claims by China.

What is less understood in the West is that China's maritime ambitions extend across the entire globe.

China needs vast resources to supply its population with food and energy, and the Chinese feel that they must be able to compete for control of the world's oceans at any time. China has not openly discussed this view with the international media or through diplomatic channels. For foreign consumption, the party line is that China's maritime ambitions are limited to the East China Sea. However, these global ambitions are well-documented internally in China, and it is thoroughly understood that the goal is to dominate all the world's oceans. This might seem like a wild ambition, even for the people who built the Great Wall by hand, but it is not terribly different from the Great Britain's drive to "rule the waves" or the naval domination the United States achieved subsequent to WWII.

China's intentions are more than the usual infamous grandiose claims of all communist governments. They have begun to make manifest what they see as their maritime destiny. China is currently building port facilities for its Navy and Maritime fleets in Pakistan and Africa. China also invested heavily in the Panama Canal, and in 1997, the Panamanian government, in violation of its canal treaty with the United States, granted control of the Panama Canal operations to the Hong Kong company Hutchison Whampoa. The administration of US President Clinton was in the midst of major military budget cuts and chose not to take issue with the Panamanian government over the treaty violation.

Under the Torrijos-Carter Treaty, the United States had the right to retake control of the Panama Canal to prevent it from falling under control of any nation other than Panama. The United States chose not to take action. Communist China now controls Hong Kong, and thus controls the Panama Canal. The same Hutchison Whampoa company now owns port facilities in Mexico and mobile phone systems in various nations through secondary companies that they directly control. You do the math.

How far China will succeed in realizing its vision of ruling the waves will depend on how well it succeeds economically at home. One of the greatest enabling factors for China's economic growth has been the decades of favorable trade that it has enjoyed with the United States, in particular, and the Western economies in general. Those decades of fantastic profits have enabled China to build a modern military and a much larger and more modern Chinese navy. It has also allowed China to upgrade its CMM.

In 2018 and 2019, the Trump administration challenged China on US-China trade relations. One of the consequences of this confrontation was that in late 2019, Chinese ship building slowed significantly and several shipyards were completely closed. Whether or not the United States will be able to achieve a more balanced trade system with China remains to be seen. Getting China to then adhere to any balanced trade system will be an even greater challenge.

TWO PROMINENT COLD WAR SPY SHIP INCIDENTS

THE FIRST US SPY SHIP INCIDENT THAT LOOMS LARGE IN AMERICA'S collective memory occurred on June 8, 1967, when Israeli jets and torpedo boats attacked the USS *Liberty*. The assault resulted in the deaths of thirty-four American sailors and civilian NSA employees and serious injuries to 171 of the surviving members of the crew. That incident remains a major diplomatic problem for Israel in her relations with the United States to this day. What happened with the USS *Liberty* requires careful examination to begin to understand what we know occurred, and to question what we are uncertain about.

The second major US spy ship incident that remains an angry memory for many Americans occurred less than seven months after Israel assaulted the USS *Liberty*. On January 23, 1968, North Korean Dictator Kim Il Sung ordered the North Korean Navy to attack and capture the USS *Pueblo*, an unarmed US Navy spy ship. The North Koreans claim that the *Pueblo* entered North Korean waters. The Pueblo crew and the US Navy maintain that the USS *Pueblo* was and had been in international waters when a North Korean patrol boat set upon it.

Due to the intense news coverage of the USS *Liberty* and the USS *Pueblo*, they are what most Westerners remember about US spy ships of the modern era. Because they constituted 96 percent of what the average voter knew about US spy ship operations at the time, the USS *Liberty* and USS *Pueblo* incidents had a disproportionate impact on US foreign policy for several years after they occurred. Information released in recent years such as White House records, US Navy records, interviews with Admiral Kidd, statements from Israelis, and other documents helped us to flesh out the events as we walk through those incidents in the next two sections.

10

USS LIBERTY INCIDENT

IN 1967, EGYPT BLOCKADED ISRAELI SHIPS FROM THE PORT OF Aqaba in Jordan. Syria, Egypt, and Jordan mobilized, along with part of the Iraqi Army. This was accompanied by weeks of public announcements from the leaders of Jordan, Syria, and Egypt that they intended to annihilate Israel and all the Jews there within. Israel was forced into war.

On June 5, 1967, Israel attacked and severely damaged the Egyptian Air Force. Then Israel followed up that air attack with a successful campaign against a vastly numerically superior Egyptian Army in the Sinai desert. It came to be known as the Six Days War. The planned annihilation of Israel was not going well for the Arab armies. The Six Days War, the events leading up to it, and the aftermath are fascinating topics for any writer, but our intention is to deal specifically with Israel's greatest failure during the Six Days War, the USS *Liberty* incident.

On June 8, 1967, Israeli aircraft and torpedo boats attacked a clearly-marked US Navy signals intelligence ship, the USS *Liberty*, while she was underway in international waters off the coast of Sinai. The surviving crew members of the USS *Liberty* remain certain that the attack was deliberate and done with the knowledge of Israel, and that the ship was a neutral American ship in international waters. Israel maintains that the attack was deliberate, but that it was the result of mistaken identity. Make no mistake about it. Over fifty years later, the attack on the USS *Liberty* remains a major controversy for all those concerned, and it does so for a variety of reasons and agendas.

The conduct of the USS *Liberty* on June 8, 1967, is fairly easy to understand. To try to understand the decisions made by then US President Lyndon Johnson, as well as his possible motives and the motives of the Israelis, we must examine the circumstances and events leading up to the attack.

Before we consider that complex web of facts and weed out the mountains of both deliberate and accidental misinformation, we must first acknowledge the remarkable courage of the men of the USS *Liberty* and their outstanding seamanship, which enabled them to keep their damaged ship afloat and underway long enough to reach a repair facility in Malta. While the USS *Liberty* incident remains a heated controversy for many and an angry recollection for the US Navy, the United States can remember the conduct of her captain and crew with pride.

A timeline surrounding the attack on the USS *Liberty* is useful in understanding the complex events that led to it, the state of mind of President Lyndon Johnson, and the attitude of the Israelis. It also helps dispel some of the obvious misinformation that has surfaced since the attack occurred. General Sherman was right when he said that war is hell, and someone in Germany was right when they coined the phrase, "The devil is in the details." If there is indeed a devil, he was certainly present and active in the details surrounding the attack on the USS *Liberty*.

TIMELINE—BEFORE THE ATTACK

MARCH 8, 1965

Egyptian President Abdel Nasser, encouraged by military support and promises of "solidarity" from the Soviet Union, announced, "We shall not enter Palestine with its soil covered in sand. We shall enter it with its soil saturated in blood." The Soviets did, in fact, support Egypt generously in the form of weapons, cash, training, and engineering projects. The solidarity had yet to arrive.

January-March 1967

Terrorists launched over 250 attacks against Israel from Syria, resulting in tank and artillery duels.

February 22, 1967

Syrian President al-Attassi made a public plea to the Arab world to "move from the defensive to the offensive to liberate the usurped land."

April 7, 1967

Syrian Artillery batteries once more fired on Israeli farmers from the Golan Heights. This time, Israel reacted, and Israeli jets attack the Syrian gun positions. Syrian Mig 21s entered the fray with a result that became a set pattern over the ensuing decades —six Syrian jets were shot down with no Israeli losses.

April 8, 1967

Syria announced that it would battle the Israelis "until the Zionist presence is ended."

May 2, 1967

The USS *Liberty* put to sea from Norfolk, Virginia. It was tasked with gathering intelligence from the west coast of Africa.

May 11, 1967

UN Secretary General U Thant delivered a speech about "the grave situation in the Mideast," but he offered no solution.

May 13, 1967

Egyptian General Anwar Sadat returned to Egypt from a trip to Russia. He informed President Nasser that Soviet intelligence confirmed the Israelis had massed twelve army brigades—approximately 20,000 troops—on the Syrian border for a surprise invasion of Syria. The Soviets had lied to General Sadat. So much for the solidarity.

Soviet Union General Secretary Leonid Brezhnev was in the process of formulating an armed intervention into his Warsaw Pact "allies." His intent was to crack down on "the liberalism that Khrushchev had allowed to fester." The Soviet Union wanted the United States and Europe preoccupied with as many other crises as possible when it launched that crack down the next year, so the Soviet Union's goal in the Middle East at that time was to foster unrest as a distraction for the West. The relationship with Sadat was collateral damage. . . . Let the solidarity flow.

Anwar Sadat never forgot that Soviet betrayal. The road to Camp David started in Moscow.

May 14, 1967

Israel intercepted and decoded an alert message transmitted to the Egyptian Army by its headquarters. Egypt flaunted its mobilization of armored units by parading them through the streets of Cairo in front of foreign correspondents and diplomats.

May 15, 1967

Israel reinforced the Sinai and sent a message that it was doing so in defense and did not intend to invade Egypt.

May 16, 1967

As Egyptian armored forces approached the Israeli border, Egyptian President Nasser demanded that the UN peacekeeping force of 3400 soldiers depart from the area.

The Joint Chiefs of Staff and the US Intelligence Community informed US President Lyndon Johnson that Egypt would invade Israel with 90,000 troops, and that Syria and Jordan would join in the attack.

Cairo Radio began broadcasting announcements that the time for Israel's demise had come. They continued for several weeks.

May 17, 1967

UN Secretary U Thant informed Egypt that there was no recent buildup of Israeli forces.

May 18, 1967

Without conferring with the UN Security Council, U Thant ordered the UN peacekeeping force to depart from the Sinai.

On May 19, and while still May 18 in Washington, DC, the UN forces left the Sinai. The United Kingdom loudly protested the withdrawal of the UN forces without any agreement by UN members. If Israel wondered about the United Nation's value prior to May 19, 1967, it has had little reason to wonder since then.

May 20, 1967

The United States ordered her Sixth Fleet, including two carrier strike forces comprising Task Force 60, to remain at least 100 miles west of Egypt.

Note: It is critical to remember that the USS *Liberty* was not operationally part of Sixth Fleet.

May 22, 1967

Egyptian President Nasser announced that no Israeli ships would be allowed to reach the port of Aqaba on the Red Sea. With Egyptian batteries now occupying the heights above Aqaba that were previously occupied by the UN forces, Israel could not receive the usual oil shipments from Iran, and the Israeli Army could not maneuver without oil. Israel had to seek a victory before the oil ran out. Israel called up her reserves, but Israeli reservists could not remain out of their civilian jobs for long without crippling the Israeli economy. The clock was ticking.

President Lyndon Johnson condemned Egypt for blockading an international waterway at the straits of Tiran. The United States and the United Kingdom ordered all of their citizens to leave the area.

The USS *Liberty* made the port of Abidjan, Ivory Coast for a four-day port call.

May 23, 1967

The NSA requested that the Joint Chiefs of Staff task the USS *Liberty* with gathering signals intelligence from a position in international waters off of Port Said, Egypt.

May 24, 1967

The USS *Liberty* departed from the Ivory Coast and made for US Naval Station Rota, Spain at "best speed."

Israeli Foreign Minister Abba Eban departed for a public relations trip to France and the United Kingdom.

UN Secretary General U Thant went to Cairo to talk to Nasser to try to calm things down. He was apparently quite the optimist.

Egyptian Minister of War Shams Badran departed Cairo for Moscow for the only reason any Middle Eastern official goes to Moscow—to ask for money, free weapons, and support. He was apparently another optimist.

Canada and Denmark requested that the UN Security Council convene an emergency meeting to try to prevent a war.

The UK carrier HMS *Victorious* took in her lines to depart for England, but was then ordered to remain in Malta on alert.

Jordan announced that Iraqi and Saudi forces were being deployed to Jordan to pre-position for war with Israel.

May 25, 1967

Cairo Radio announced, "The Arab peoples firmly resolved to wipe Israel off the map."

The UK carrier HMS *Hermes* was recalled from Singapore to Aden.

May 26, 1967

Israeli Foreign Minister Eban met with President Johnson at the White House.

May 27, 1967

The US European Command ordered the Sixth Fleet to keep all her aircraft a minimum distance of 100 miles from Egypt and Syria.

May 28, 1967

US Secretary of State Dean Rusk informed Israel that the United States, United Kingdom, Canada, and The Netherlands were preparing a plan to escort oil tankers through the straits of Tiran to Aqaba.

May 29, 1967

The NSA sent "tasking" information to the USS *Liberty*. In English, that meant that the *Liberty* was told where and on what it should concentrate her signals intelligence efforts.

May 30, 1967

The Soviet Union announced that it would reinforce its Mediterranean fleet.

June 1, 1967

The USS *Liberty* made port in Rota, Spain. The ship resupplied, and it took on equipment and several more intelligence specialists.

June 2, 1957

The USS *Liberty* departed Rota, Spain, headed for the coast of Egypt.

June 3, 1967

The devil was in the details and in Nasser's ear. In another display of warm Soviet solidarity, the Soviet Ambassador to Egypt assured Egyptian President Nasser that Israel would be unable to resist.

June 4, 1967

The Israeli Cabinet voted to go to war.

Egypt sent two commando battalions to Jordan and moved them to the Israeli border.

June 5, 1967

Israel conducted effective air strikes against Egyptian air bases and all but destroyed the Egyptian Air Force.

June 6, 1967

Israel, as well as other countries, intercepted a call between President Nasser of Egypt and King Hussein of Jordan in which the two of them agreed to claim that UK and US aircraft had been flying combat missions for Israel. Radio Cairo dutifully broadcasted the fictitious claim. Radio Beirut and Radio Amman quickly followed suit. The Soviet Union joined in with the same misinformation broadcast across the Soviet Union and Eastern Europe. Egypt was not about to admit that the Israeli Air force caught the Egyptian Air Force napping on the eve of war.

Nasser should have been asking himself why his pals in the Soviet KGB, who always claimed to know so much about Israeli intentions, missed this one. A smarter person would have asked that question, but Nasser was not a "smarter person." He was just Nasser.

June 7, 1967

The annihilation of Israel was not going as planned and was starting to look like it might be the Egyptian and Jordanian armies that would be annihilated. The Soviet Union asked for an emergency session of the UN Security Council and proposed an immediate cease fire. Jordan informed the UN that it agreed to the cease fire proposal.

President Johnson sent a HOTLINE message to Moscow, pointing out that Syria and Egypt had not agreed to a cease fire. He also pointed out that they had broken off diplomatic relations, that they were failing to protect US citizens and embassy personnel, and that the consequences may be grave.

The NSA requested that the USS *Liberty* change her operational area to further west off of the coast of Egypt due to the rapid western advance of the Israeli Army.

Are you a bit confused yet with the complexity of the events? You should be. Things were changing at a fast pace during early June of 1967.

Keep in mind that all of this was happening while President Johnson was almost completely absorbed by the US "non-war" in Vietnam and increasingly distracted by the growing anti-war protests at home. Also, President Johnson insisted on pursuing a severe micromanagement strategy concerning the Vietnam War, and he often went without much sleep as he attempted to personally control every air strike and minute detail about the land forces in Southeast Asia. His probable exhaustion resulting from his mania for micromanagement likely impacted how he handled the events of June 8, 1967.

June 8, 1967

As the sun rose over the Middle East on the morning of June 8, 1967, the fortunes of Israel seemed much improved as compared to a week earlier. Before the sun set again, the relationship between Israel and the United States would change forever.

The Egyptian and Jordanian armies were in shambles. The Syrian, Egyptian, and Jordanian air forces were almost completely destroyed. Israel had captured Jerusalem, the West Bank, the Sinai Desert, and the Gaza Strip. The Israeli war cabinet was debating whether or not to invade the Syrian Golan Heights.

The Israeli Command Room busily attempted to keep an accurate picture of its force dispositions and the locations and intentions of military units in the theater of combat. For five days, the updates to the main map table had been almost completely favorable to the Israeli military. Not having been in that room ourselves and not having any reliable sources who *were* in that room, we can only guess that the tension preceding the war and any anxiety in its early hours was gradually replaced by relief and confidence as the markers representing various Egyptian and Jordanian army units were removed from the map table.

TIMELINE—JUNE 8 ATTACK ON THE USS *LIBERTY*

MANY INDIVIDUALS FROM MANY NATIONS PLAYED A PART IN THE events leading up to the June 8, 1967 attack on the USS *Liberty*. Times of events were recorded in a variety of time zones. For our purposes, we will use 24 hour "Zulu" time. US military communications are generally logged in "Zulu," or what Englishmen call Greenwich Mean Time.

0110Z

The US Joint Chiefs of Staff released a Top Secret written "standoff" message to the Army Communications Center ordering the USS *Liberty* to remain at least 100 miles from the coasts of Egypt, Israel, and Syria. It was meant for transmission to the US Commander of US Forces in Europe. We will call this message "080110Z."

0210Z

The Israeli Air Force launched a routine dawn reconnaissance flight to patrol her coastal area.

0211Z

Message 080110Z, now encrypted, was transmitted to the US Commander of European Forces, General Lemnitzer. The message was received and decoded.

0312Z

The Commander of US Naval Forces Europe, Admiral John McCain, received Message 080110Z.

These days, it can be confusing as to which "John McCain" was in command of our US Naval Forces in Europe in 1967. At the time, Senator John McCain, the son of Admiral John McCain, was in a

POW camp in Hanoi, North Vietnam. Senator John McCain was not involved with the USS *Liberty* incident.

0315Z

Ensign J.D. Scott had the deck watch on the USS *Liberty*. He observed a "flying boxcar" aircraft circling off the port beam of the ship. He was unable to see any identifying marks on the plane with his binoculars.

0350Z

Israeli Naval headquarters ("HQ") in Haifa received a message from the flying boxcar that a ship that might be a destroyer was sailing toward Gaza on compass heading 120 degrees True. The Israeli Command Room staff designated the USS *Liberty* as a "skunk," meaning unknown, and placed a red marker for it on the map table.

At the same time, the Army Communications Center in the Pentagon transmitted the 080110Z standoff message to the USS *Liberty* and to the Sixth Fleet. The *Liberty* did not receive the message.

0400Z

The Israeli Navy ordered Motor Torpedo Boats ("MTB's") to standby to put to sea.

0403Z

The Israeli Navy received a message from its flying boxcar updating the contact with the USS *Liberty* as a "US supply ship."

If Israeli Intelligence had already received information about the previous US standoff orders sent to Sixth Fleet and the new message intended for the USS *Liberty*, they might have wondered why a US Navy supply ship was in the area. What, if any, information Israeli Intelligence received from inside the Pentagon at the time is unknown to us, and the Israelis are not going to tell us or anyone else. We can only wonder. However, Holmes is guessing that the Israeli spies inside of the Soviet system were not yet picking up Soviet intercepts of US Navy traffic, as the Walker Spy Ring* did not deliver US Navy encryption information to the Soviets until the following year.

0649Z

USS *Liberty* took a westerly heading when she turned to course 259 degrees True.

0650Z

USS *Liberty* reported being orbited by two delta wing aircraft. They were too far away for identification.

0700Z

Major General Schlomo Erell, Commander of the Israeli Navy, was informed that the 0350Z contact was still designated as a "skunk" with a red marker on the map table. He ordered the marker changed to green for neutral.

An Israeli Air Force air controller received a message from a pilot that he was fired on by a ship near El Arish. The Israeli Navy dispatched two destroyers to the area to search for Egyptian warships.

0705Z

The USS *Liberty* reduced speed to 5 knots to "loiter" off the Egyptian coast in international waters.

0740Z

After the "fired upon" Israeli pilot landed and was questioned, the Israeli Air Force was not convinced that he was fired on by a ship at all. The pilot's description of the ship fit that of the USS

Liberty. The Israeli destroyers were ordered to reverse course back to their original patrol area further north and further away from the *Liberty's* position.

0855Z

After the flying boxcar patrol craft landed and the crew was debriefed, the Israeli naval intelligence branch, NID, informed the Israeli Navy HQ that the ship spotted earlier was the USS *Liberty*.

0856Z

The *Liberty* recorded another flying boxcar plane circling. No markings were observed.

The *Liberty* reported to US Naval Security Station Command that due to the current situation, she had taken the precaution of destroying all superseded messages.

0900Z

The Israeli Naval HQ duty officer ordered the green marker for the USS *Liberty* removed from the board as an old contact.

0917Z

US Navy Admiral Martin ordered another standoff message to be sent to USS *Liberty* with a "received message" answer requested. *Liberty* did not receive the message until after the attack.

0920Z

Israeli MTB Division 914 ("MTB 914") consisting of three MTB's sailed from Ashdod for a patrol to Ashkelon.

0924Z

The Israeli Navy received reports that a ship was shelling El Arish.

0926Z

USS *Liberty* recorded that yet another patrol craft was circling her.

0927Z

Israeli Defense Force Central Command in Tel Aviv received a report that a ship was shelling El Arish.

0938Z

USS *Liberty* changed course to 238 degrees True.

0945Z

Tel Aviv received another message of "ship activity" off El Arish.

0955Z

USS *Liberty* recorded sighting an explosion in the El Arish area. Apparently, the retreating Egyptian Army was exploding ammo dumps rather than allowing their capture by the rapidly-advancing Israeli Army.

0958Z

The Israeli Naval HQ recorded a semi-legible entry describing two targets firing on El Arish.

1005Z

Israeli Navy Captain Rehav ordered MTB 914 to patrol north of El Arish.

1015Z

MTB 914 received the order to proceed to the El Arish area.

1110Z

USS *Liberty* went to General Quarters (battle stations) as a drill.

1117Z

Israeli MTB 914 was informed of reports of shelling off of El Arish.

1130Z

Liberty recorded another explosion in the El Arish area. The Israeli MTB squadron was again informed that El Arish was being shelled from the sea.

1141Z

Israeli MTB 914 detected the USS *Liberty* on its WWI-era radar.

1145Z

Israeli MTB 914 was ordered to close with the contact and identify it.

1147Z

MTB 914 reported to Israeli Navy HQ that the "target is making 30 knots" and requested air support since they would be unable to catch the target.

The maximum speed of the USS *Liberty* under ideal conditions was 18 knots. The MTB crew had misinterpreted their radar data and had wildly miscalculated the speed of the *Liberty*. The higher speed that they reported led the Israeli Navy HQ to suspect that MTB 914 was tracking a warship.

1148Z

The Israeli Navy requested air support from the Israeli Air Force.

The USS *Liberty* secured from General Quarters drill, and the Captain ordered the *Liberty* left in "condition three," which meant most of her watertight hatchways closed except when a crew member was passing through the hatchway. *Liberty*, which had modern radar, took a radar fix on the El Arish minaret and verified that the ship was 25.5 miles away from shore in international waters.

1150Z

Israeli MTB 914 reported that the target was 17 miles distance making 28 knots. This message, when compared to previous reports, should have caused the commander of MTB 914 and the Israeli Naval HQ to realize that MTB 914 was mistaken in its reporting of the speed and position of the target, as the ship sighted could not have traveled that fast.

1151Z

USS *Liberty* recorded a radar contact of three small ships at 16 knots distance. It was MTB 914.

1154Z

An Israeli flight of two fighters with call sign "Kursa" reported having "the ship" in sight.

Flight "Royal," a flight of two Dassault Mystère IV attack planes armed with napalm and headed for the Sinai, were diverted to the *Liberty's* position.

1158Z

Kursa flight attacked the USS *Liberty* with 20mm cannon fire and rockets. Captain McGonagle was on the bridge at the time of the attack. Bleeding and badly wounded, he remained on the bridge.

1201Z

MTB 914 was ordered to proceed fast to target.

1202Z

Israeli Royal flight was given permission to attack.

1203Z

USS *Liberty* recorded explosion on port side. Napalm detonated on the deck of the *Liberty* and poured into the interior through rocket and cannon holes made by the attacking aircraft. Her communications antennas had been destroyed.

1204Z

Kursa flight left the attack site and Royal flight attacked the USS *Liberty*.

1205Z

USS *Liberty* went to General Quarters. Captain McGonagle ordered flank speed.

1206

MTB 914 reported it was 11 knots from the "target" and requested that aircraft leave the area.

1209Z

Israeli Air Force HQ asked for the target ship's identity to be checked.

1210Z

US carrier USS *Saratoga* of Sixth Fleet received a message from *Liberty* that she was under attack. The *Liberty* had been transmitting the message repeatedly since 1158Z.

Later, during a US Navy Court of Inquiry conducted by Admiral Kidd, the *Liberty's* communications specialists testified that their communications channels were being jammed. This and the fact that the attacking Israeli aircraft destroyed her antennas would explain the delay in transmitting a message concerning the attack.

Many individuals have attempted to refute the jamming claim made by the *Liberty* crew members. It should be remembered that all crew members of the USS *Liberty* were handpicked by the Navy and vetted for Secret and Top Secret clearances. In addition, Captain McGonagle reviewed service records, and based on his impression of any crew member, he could have had them replaced at any time.

The communications specialists on the *Liberty* were well-trained, well-tested Navy radiomen and communications technicians with established reputations for efficiency, accuracy, and integrity. Civilian NSA employees on board the *Liberty* at the time of the attack were also handpicked and well-vetted by the NSA. The notion that the USS *Liberty* communications team was mistaken about having its primary communications frequencies actively jammed defies all logic and reason.

1211Z

MTB 914 reported that they were on their attack run. Royal flight reported that the target ship had an identifier of "Charlie Tango Romeo Five" (CTR-5). The *Liberty* was actually marked GTR 5.

1212Z

The Israeli Air Force controllers suspected that the ship might be American and ordered their aircraft to leave the area.

1213Z

Israeli Air Force dispatched two helicopters to the scene to rescue survivors.

1217Z

Israeli Navy HQ ordered MTB 914 *not* to attack, and that identification of the target might be mistaken. Later, MTB 914

Commander Oren claimed he didn't receive the order to halt the attack, but the order was recorded in his boat's log.

1226Z

USS *Liberty* crew noticed that her flag had been shot away in the air attacks. They hoisted the 7' X 13' Holiday Flag—a larger version of the American flag used for diplomatic entries into ports and other special events.

1228Z

USS *Liberty* log indicates a flashing light from the attacking MTB's, but the *Liberty's* signal lamps were destroyed by the Israeli air attacks, and the ship was unable to signal back.

1230Z

One of the *Liberty's* 50 caliber machine gun mounts opened fire on the attacking MTB's. Captain McGonagle ordered "cease fire" because he suspected that the MTB's were Israeli and were attacking in error. Another machine gun fired, but it was later determined that it fired spontaneously due to heat from the napalm-induced fire.

1230Z to 1232Z

The times of the log entries of the USS *Liberty* and those of the log entries of MTB 914 differ by a few minutes. Commander Orem of MTB 914 reported that the target ship was the Egyptian *El Quseir*.

The *Liberty* bears no resemblance to that Egyptian ship. The standard method for describing a ship's size is to state the weight of the water that the ship displaces when it is afloat. The *El Quseir* was a third of the size of the *Liberty* and had a displacement of 2,600 tons. The USS *Liberty* displaced 7,700 tons. The *Liberty* had distinctive satellite antennas clearly visible above her decks. The *El Quseir's* profile was quite different from that of the USS *Liberty*.

After reporting that they were being fired on and asking several times for permission to attack, Israeli Naval HQ gave permission to MTB 914 to attack the USS *Liberty*.

1232Z

Rear Admiral Geis took tactical command of Task Force 60, which was the main battle component of Sixth Fleet.

1234Z

USS *Liberty* attempted to maneuver to avoid oncoming torpedoes. A torpedo passed astern of the *Liberty*.

1235Z

An Israeli torpedo hit USS *Liberty* amidships on her starboard side, blasting a hole approximately 40 feet in diameter into her hull. *Liberty* rapidly began taking on water. The torpedo damaged the electrical system and the *Liberty* lost electrical power.

1236Z

The *USS Liberty* lost steam pressure and secured her boilers. She was dead in the water. At this point, with 34 crew members dead or dying and 171 crew members wounded including the captain, no reasonable person would have given good odds for the *Liberty* remaining afloat for long. Reasonable betters would have lost that bet.

Remarkably, the remaining crew members managed to perform brilliant damage control work. They eventually regained electrical power, controlled the fires and flooding, and got the ship underway.

We would note that the only doctor on board the USS *Liberty* was Navy Doctor Richard Kiefer. He was badly wounded in the attack, suffering a broken right knee cap and an open wound to his left leg, and he had eleven pieces of shrapnel in his abdomen. He bound his abdomen together with a life jacket and proceeded to tend to his wounded shipmates non-stop for over 24 hours. Thanks to his remarkable courage, determination, and skill, many of the *Liberty's* wounded were kept alive.

1238Z

The aircraft carrier USS *Saratoga* received a radio message from the *Liberty* stating that she was under attack and badly damaged. The message was sent "in clear," meaning it was not coded.

1239Z

The Israeli Air Force helicopters heading for the USS *Liberty* were told that the ship was an Israeli cargo ship.

1240Z

USS *Liberty* recorded that one of the attacking torpedo boats had hull number 206.

1250Z

Commander of Task Force 60, Admiral Martin, ordered the USS *Saratoga* to launch four armed A-1 attack planes to go to the aid of the *Liberty*. The next day, he apologized to Admiral Geis for not issuing the order through him due to the urgency of the situation.

MTB 914 was ordered to search for survivors and identify the attacked ship.

1251Z

MTB 914 reported to Israeli Naval Command that the ship "might be Russian."

1256Z

The Israeli Air Force helicopters were ordered to identify and report the languages which were spoken by any of the rescued seamen.

1307Z

USS *Liberty* identified helicopters with Israeli markings circling her.

1311Z

The National Military Command in the Pentagon received a message from the US Commander Europe reporting the attack on the *Liberty*.

1312Z

The Israeli helicopter pilots informed the Israeli Air Force that the attacked ship was American and flying a United States flag.

1314Z

The Pentagon informed the NSA of the attack on USS *Liberty*. During the attack, a US Navy NSA-controlled EC121 aircraft had been routinely recording communications traffic in the area of the attack.

1316Z

US Naval Task Force 60 Tactical Commander Admiral Geis ordered the re-transmission of Admiral Martin's message to the carriers USS *America* and USS *Saratoga* with an ASAP and a reminder that "defend the *Liberty* means just that."

1319Z

Power was restored to the bridge and the fires were extinguished but USS *Liberty* remained unable to steer.

1320Z

Israeli MTB Division 914 reported to Israeli Naval Command that the ship was American, and that the fires aboard had been extinguished.

1330Z

US Admiral Martin reported that US Navy Task Force 60 was headed toward the last reported position of the USS *Liberty* at 27 knots.

1346Z

Israeli MTB 914 was ordered to proceed to El Arish.

1348Z

Soviet First Deputy Premier Alexi Kosygin sent a HOTLINE message to US President Johnson concerning a UN-proposed cease fire between Israel and the Arab states.

1355Z

USS *Liberty* recorded that she had re-established communications. Her radio log indicated that she was only able to transmit, not receive, and only on her high frequency voice radio equipment, as opposed to encrypted teletype messages, short range tactical communications equipment, etc.

1400Z

Israeli Defense Forces informed US Naval Attaché Commander Ernest Castle of the attack on the USS *Liberty* due to "mistaken identity." After visiting the Israeli headquarters commander, Castle sent Flash Messages to the White House and Sixth Fleet reporting that the Israelis said a tragic accident had occurred. Israel did not deny that it attacked; it denied that the attack was intentional.

1401Z

The *Liberty* radio indicated that she could now both transmit and receive voice messages at high frequency.

The USS *Saratoga* launched four A-1s to defend the USS *Liberty*.

The thirty-nine minutes required for launch seems excessive by modern carrier operation standards, but USS *Saratoga* had been conducting nuclear launch drills for nuclear armed planes when she received the order to launch the A-1s. Before she could do that, she had to secure from the nuclear launch drills using rigidly-enforced and precise sequences of procedures due to the handling of nuclear weapons.

1405Z

USS *Liberty* transmitted a report on her condition and an initial casualty list.

1410Z

US Navy Task Force 63 recommended that fleet tug USS *Papago* be dispatched to assist the *Liberty*.

1411Z

USS *Liberty* recorded that small vessels were approaching her again.

1416Z

US Joint Chiefs of Staff sent a message to Commander US Forces Europe that the use of force was authorized. Note that Admirals Martin and Geis had already effectively authorized use of force.

1425Z

Sixth Fleet messaged the US European Command that they were not currently in communication with the USS *Liberty*. US Navy communications centers in Morocco and Greece were able to copy transmissions from the *Liberty*.

1426Z

Sixth Fleet re-established communications with the *Liberty* via the US Navy communications center in Greece.

1430Z

USS *Liberty* reported to Sixth Fleet that she was making 8 knots under her own power on a heading of 340 degrees True.

1433Z

Israeli MTB 914 approached the *Liberty* and, via megaphone, offered "assistance." The *Liberty* declined.

1438Z

Commander US Naval Forces Europe, Admiral McCain, received a message from the US Defense Attaché in Tel Aviv explaining that the Israelis asserted that the incident was a tragic mistake.

1439Z

Admiral Martin messaged Admiral McCain that all aircraft were being recalled.

1440Z

Admiral Martin transmitted a recall order to both the USS *America* and the USS *Saratoga*.

1500Z

The *Liberty* stopped her engines again.

Deputy Secretary of Defense Cyrus Vance called Admiral McCain on a telephone and informed him that all news releases concerning the USS *Liberty* incident would come from Washington, not from the ships.

1502Z

Admiral Martin transmitted another situational report indicating that two destroyers were proceeding at best speed to the USS *Liberty*.

1506Z

President Johnson arrived at the White House to join an emergency meeting. Secretary of Defense Robert McNamara, Secretary of State Dean Rusk, Chairman, Foreign Intelligence Adviser Clark Clifford, Under Secretary of State Nicholas Katzenbach, Ambassador to Russia Llewellen Thompson, Special Consultant McGeorge Bundy, and National Security Advisor W. W. Rostow were all at the meeting.

1510Z

US Ambassador to Israel Walworth Barbour messaged the State Dept. that "the Israelis are obviously shocked by the error."

1525Z

US Defense Secretary McNamara called the Pentagon and ordered that the aircraft sent to aid the USS *Liberty* be recalled. They had already been recalled by Admiral Martin forty-five minutes earlier.

1529Z

The Joint Chiefs of Staff transmitted a message stating that the previous use of force order had been withdrawn.

1530Z

The Defense Department issued its first press release concerning the attack on the USS *Liberty*, stating that an accident had occurred and the Israelis mistakenly attacked a US ship.

1600Z

USS *Liberty* reported that she was under way and having difficulty maintaining a course.

1710Z

Israeli Prime Minister Eshkol convened a cabinet meeting to discuss a possible Israeli attack on, and occupation of, the Golan Heights on the Israeli-Syrian border. Defense Minister Dayan and others were against the attack. The meeting convened without an agreement.

1730Z

Radio Cairo transmitted a report that the USS *Liberty's* position close to the coast of Egypt was proof of US direct assistance to Israel in the war. Unfortunately, some Egyptians still believe that nonsensical report.

1900Z

UN Secretary General U Thant read the "United Arab Republic" acceptance of a UN-proposed cease fire.

June 9, 1967

0425Z

USS *Liberty* recorded that she had rendezvoused with the destroyers USS *Massey* and USS *Davis*.

0436Z

UN Secretary General received a message from Syria agreeing to the cease fire. Israeli records indicate that the Syrians were still shelling Israel from the Golan Heights at this time. The Syrians claim they were not.

0500Z

Israeli Defense Minister Dayan ordered the Israeli Defense Forces Northern Command to attack and seize the Golan Heights.

0930Z

Israeli UN representatives informed the Secretary General that Syria had continued to shell Israel from the Golan Heights and that the Israeli military had entered the Golan Heights to silence the guns.

1510Z

The USS *Papago* reached the *Liberty*. The Sixth Fleet tug *Papago*, the destroyer *Davis,* and the *Liberty* were ordered to proceed to Crete. Later, they were ordered to proceed to Malta where a dry dock was available.

1531Z

President Johnson received a HOTLINE message from Soviet Vice Premier Kosygin threatening Soviet military action against Israel if it did not halt its advance into the Golan Heights.

1630Z

Israel and Syria agreed to a final cease fire. The Six Day War ended.

---

*See *Spycraft: Essentials* for more on the Walker Family Spy Ring.

13

AFTERMATH OF USS LIBERTY ATTACK

MANY IN THE UNITED STATES, INCLUDING THE CREW OF THE USS *Liberty*, former US Secretary of State Dean Rusk, Admiral Isaac Kidd, Jr., Admiral Thomas Moorer, former NSA Director General William Odom, several NSA executives with access to transcripts of the Israeli aircraft's communications, then CIA Director Richard Helms, several members of Congress, and a slew of academicians consistently maintain that the attack on the USS *Liberty* was conducted by Israel with the knowledge that they were attacking a US ship. Not everyone agrees. Some Americans feel that accusing Israel of knowingly attacking a US ship is simply "anti-Israeli/anti-Semitic" bigotry.

The Israeli apologists are not all of like mind in their positions. Some claim that the attack was, indeed, an accident, but they acknowledge that people may disagree without holding anti-Israeli motives. Others cite imaginary conclusions from imaginary investigations and unsubstantiated evidence showing that the entire matter was the fault of the USS *Liberty* and the US Navy. The crew of the USS *Liberty* have consistently resisted any association with various radical groups that attempt to use the USS *Liberty* tragedy for pro-Israeli and anti-Israeli agendas.

Holmes is not a USS *Liberty* veteran, nor was he involved in any facet of the events surrounding the attack on the ship. He makes no attempt to speak on their behalf. They speak on their own behalf.   We encourage all readers to visit the USS *Liberty* Veterans Association web page at USSLiberty.org.

Some of the groups and individuals that are certain that Israel knowingly attacked a US Navy ship propose interesting and often fantastic conspiracy theories concerning the motives of Israel and of the United States. Some people claim that President Johnson and/or others in the United States cooperated with Israel to arrange the entire attack as an excuse to enter the war against Egypt, Syria, and Jordan.

Holmes disagrees with these theories. For one thing, the United States already had an excuse to enter the war as soon as Egypt restricted international traffic through the Straits of Tiran to international navigation. For another, if Israel wanted to attack a known US ship to drag the United States into the war, it could have done so more effectively earlier on that day rather than waiting. By the time of the attack on the *Liberty,* the Arabs had already lost so there was no urgency to get the United States into the war.

US President Johnson already had his hands full with the micro-mismanagement of the Vietnam conflict. The United States was maintaining a strong military presence in Europe, Japan, Okinawa, the Philippines, and Korea in order to contain communist aggression. Johnson was clearly not seeking a new war to mismanage. In fact, he soon grew so tired of dealing with the Cold War, the Vietnam non-war, his own political party, the "other" political party, and the US media that he decided not to seek re-election.

Also, if the United States had wanted to enter a war against "the Arabs," we probably would not have entered one against three petroleum-poor nations such as Egypt, Syria, and Jordan. It would have been a simple matter for the United States to stage an attack on an American ship in order to have one more of many reasons for attacking Egypt or Syria. For a simple comparison, please refer to the Tonkin Gulf incident of 1964, in which no US sailors were killed.

Other groups claim that Israel was motivated by the need to keep secret its intentions to invade the Golan Heights. This theory seems less outlandish to Holmes, but in his view, it would require some qualification. He is more willing to accept this theory as possible if he views it as a limited conspiracy on the Israeli side that did not include the entire Israeli cabinet and military command structure.

Some individuals claim that after the attack on the USS *Liberty* occurred, there was a deliberate cover-up by the US government. Holmes believes that there was. Where he disagrees with these various theories is about who orchestrated the cover-up.

President Johnson was in charge. Individuals outside the White House lacked the means and opportunity to effect a cover-up because the White House was well-informed by the NSA, the US Navy, the Pentagon, and the State Department about the available facts of the case. Johnson wanted it kept quiet and quickly forgotten for the simple reason that Israel's enemies were acting as client states for the Soviet Union, and Johnson did not wish to assist the Soviet Union by assisting Israel's enemies.

Holmes's suspicion is that members of the Israeli command structure, and perhaps a member or members of the Israeli cabinet, chose to pretend that they were uncertain of the identity of the USS *Liberty*, and they allowed a few overzealous members of the Israeli command structure to proceed with the attack. They may have been motivated by a notion that they might better keep secret their intentions toward the Golan Heights and their military operations in the theater of combat.

A congressional investigation of the matter would finally allow the surviving members of the USS *Liberty* to be heard by their government, and by not investigating, the US government assists the wildest of conspiracy theorists in supporting the most outrageous claims. By withholding the information that they have, the Israeli government is also helping to foster the most outlandish theories. Whatever or whomever those governments are protecting with silence and misinformation cannot be worth the damage to Israel's reputation and to her relations with the United States.

There are some facts surrounding the case of the *USS Liberty* that are not as easily argued against or explained as innocent mistakes. The *Liberty* crew members clearly state that their communications channels were being scrambled at the time of the attack. Israel knew that ships of the US Navy used the channels and that Egyptian freighters did not. Also, the Israeli claim that no flag was flying on the *Liberty* strikes Holmes as ridiculous.

We are all welcome to propose one or many theories. However, we suggest that to hold to a plausible theory, people should consult verifiable facts and credible testimony from the eye witnesses before forming conclusions. The easiest way to ascertain the views of the American eye witnesses is to visit the USS *Liberty* web page as indicated previously in this chapter.

On the American side, we cannot deny the lousy message handling by the US military communications networks that kept the standoff order from reaching the USS *Liberty* in time to make a difference. Had the *Liberty* received the message in time, she would have left the area of the eventual attack several hours before the attack occurred.

This in no way reduces the Israeli culpability for the attack. According to their own claims, the Israeli military attacked an unidentified ship in international waters without provocation. The Israeli government has repeatedly admitted doing so. The USS *Liberty* had every right to be where she was when the attack occurred.

Two more facts that are less subject to reasonable argument are the fact that Israeli/American relations have been impacted by the incident, as well as the fact that Israel has never shared all its information about the attack. To the degree that the growth of strong anti-Israeli sentiment can be attributed to the attack on the USS *Liberty*, it can only be blamed on the Israelis. To be sure, there are other causes of anti-Israeli sentiment in Europe and the United States that cannot be blamed on Israel, but it is within the power of the Israeli Government to mend the damage in her relations with the United States caused by Israel's attack on the USS *Liberty*.

The United States has also never shared all of its information. Three of the five tapes recorded that day are now available to listen to from the NSA. They are in Hebrew. They are not the two remaining tapes that we would really like to hear, but rather they are from before and after the actual attack. The tapes we would *like* to hear—the ones where the Israelis are actually attacking the US vessel—those two of the five tapes remain conspicuously missing. In other words, as usually occurs with the US and any other government, the "transparency" is no transparency at all to anyone except a politician.

To be clear regarding the NSA, the bureaucrats just did what they were told, and they are not to blame for the missing tapes. An article published in 2017 claims the available tapes hold shocking new revelations, but they actually do not. Find these available tapes at NSA.gov. Search on "USS Liberty Audio Tape," and the top two links will both produce a list of the available information. Click on "Audio Recordings and Transcripts" to go to the links for each of the tapes.

Regardless of what theory one ascribes to, one fact about the attack on the USS *Liberty* remains beyond any reasonable argument. The performance of the captain and crew of the *Liberty* during and after the attack was in keeping with the finest traditions of the US Navy. The USS *Liberty* remains one of the most decorated ships in the long and proud history of the US Navy, and the USS *Liberty* incident remains as an example of diligence to duty and calm courage under fire that should be understood by every young member of the US Navy. From the safety of our comfortable homes in pleasant neighborhoods, we offer a humble and sincere salute to the crew and families of the USS *Liberty*.

14

USS PUEBLO INCIDENT

FROM THE POINT OF VIEW OF THE US NAVY, THE TWO MOST notable Cold War Spy Ship incidents were the Israeli attack on the USS *Liberty* in 1967, addressed in the previous section, and the North Korean attack on the USS *Pueblo* in 1968. The USS *Pueblo* AGER-2 is a Banner class technical research ship that was originally built as a US Army cargo ship in 1944 as part of the US shipbuilding program in WWII. After the war, the *Pueblo* first operated under US Coast Guard command as a training vessel for US Army crews and then was transferred the US Navy in 1966.

The Navy took the old cargo ship and performed a low-budget conversion to a spy ship configuration by adding appropriate electronics equipment to a cramped "spook shack." Also known as "the cage," a spook shack is where the intelligence surveillance equipment is kept and where the communications and electronics personnel work. This type of low-cost conversion worked well on several ships of the same class and provided the NSA and Naval Intelligence with an economical platform for coastal electronics intelligence gathering.

After the unprovoked and still unexplained Israeli attack on the USS *Liberty* in international waters off of the coast of Egypt in 1967, we might imagine there was a rigorous evaluation and project-wide shake up that occurred in the NSA and the US Navy's spy ship program. However, that earth-shaking reorganization would take place only in our informed imaginations. Unfortunately for the crew of the USS *Pueblo*, intelligence operations continued to be conducted under NSA control without adequate coordination or support from US Navy combat fleets and air bases. For the *Pueblo* crew, the consequences of that risky strategy were horrific.

Before departing from the Puget Sound Naval Shipyard in Washington state, the Pueblo's captain, US Navy Commander Lloyd Bucher, and his intelligence specialists were concerned that the USS *Pueblo* had accumulated too many excess classified documents and manuals that were not required for their upcoming operations. The diligent Captain Bucher informed his superior officer of these materials and requested to transfer them ashore. Unfortunately, no proper storage was available for them.

Captain Bucher also requested that destruction systems be installed on all classified equipment and document storage. Unfortunately, the NSA was eager for more intelligence from the US Seventh Fleet in the Far East. As a result, the Navy, possibly under pressure from the White House, did not grant the delay needed for the installation of those simple equipment systems.

To be fair, we should disclose that we don't mind occasionally leveling a little criticism on the black hole that sucks money out of taxpayer pockets that is known as the NSA. We have never worked for them, and their highly-paid bosses like to remain silent, so they are an easy target for us. If they should take exception, they are welcome to make Holmes's computer blow up or come into his driveway for a friendly inter-agency conference.

Since we don't live in North Korea, and since the highly-paid NSA bosses are too busy counting all that cash, they won't do either. Now, back to the story . . .

Tasked with intercepting radio and radar signals and observing Soviet naval activity, the USS *Pueblo* cast off from the US Navy dock in Sasebo, Japan, on January 11, 1968. She still had unwanted classified materials aboard and still lacked any destruction system for either those materials or her code machines. An experienced, diligent officer captained her, and he commanded a well-trained, highly skilled crew. None of them would see a friendly port again for nearly a year.

At 1730 hours local time on January 21, 1968, the USS *Pueblo* was 15.5 nautical miles from the coast of North Korea near the North Korean naval base at Wonsan. Since "international waters" are twelve nautical miles (22.2 km or 13.8 miles) from the baseline, or low water mark, of a coastal state, the *Pueblo* was well within international waters, mostly listening for radar signals and generally spying from a proper distance.

At that time, a North Korean sub chaser passed within 1600 yards of the USS *Pueblo*. The sub chaser made no radio transmissions. Making an educated guess that the *Pueblo* had not yet been identified, Captain Bucher decided to continue in radio silence to further delay identification. He knew that once his vessel was identified, the North Koreans would likely reduce radio traffic.

At 2000 hours, a battle erupted on land in South Korea when a thirty-one-man North Korean infiltration team dressed as South Korean soldiers was detected and blocked at a checkpoint 100 meters from the South Korean president's residence, the Blue House. Their mission was to assassinate South Korean President Park Chung Hee. The US Navy considered the implications of the assassination attempt and decided to not recall the USS *Pueblo*.

On the next day, January 22, North Korean radio traffic increased. At approximately 1400 hours, two North Korean trawlers approached to within 500 yards of the USS *Pueblo* and then left the area. Later they returned and approached within 25 yards of the ship.

At 2000 hours, Captain Bucher transmitted Situational Report 1 to the US Navy Security Group Station in Kamiseya, Japan. Atmospheric conditions prevented that report and all other communications with Kamiseya from arriving until fourteen hours later. During the night of January 22, the Pueblo moved out to a position 50 miles offshore. In the morning, she returned to a position 25 miles off the coast of North Korea.

On January 23, 1968, Captain Bucher was lunching in the ward-room when he received a message from the bridge that a North Korean sub chaser was approaching. A few minutes later, the bridge reported that the sub chaser was making 40 knots and was within 5 miles of the *Pueblo*.

Captain Bucher sent two civilian oceanographers to take ocean samples, and the *Pueblo* raised international signal flags indicating oceanographic operations. The North Korean sub chaser transmitted a voice message to Wonsan that it was approaching an unarmed US oceanographic vessel.

The sub chaser then came within 500 yards of the USS *Pueblo* and demanded that she "heave to or be fired upon." The US ship was already laying to at the time.

The *Pueblo* took a radar range on the North Korean Coast and verified that she was 15.8 miles from North Korea. She then signaled the North Koreans that she was in international waters. Nevertheless, three North Korean P4 torpedo boats approached the USS *Pueblo* at high speed.

The USS *Pueblo* got under way and headed further from the North Korean Coast. Two North Korean Mig 21s made a low pass over the vessel. A second North Korean sub chaser and a fifth North Korean torpedo boat joined the scene.

At approximately 1330 hours, a North Korean torpedo boat attempted to come alongside and effect a boarding. The slow-moving USS *Pueblo* maneuvered to prevent that. The sub chaser opened fire with its 57mm cannon, and the torpedo boats fired their machine guns at the *Pueblo*.

Captain Bucher and another crew member on the flying bridge were wounded. The captain realized that this was not another typical harassment operation, and he ordered modified general quarters, which meant no personnel on outside deck areas. He also ordered all classified materials to be burned.

The USS *Pueblo* had two fifty-caliber machine guns. However, the ammo was below decks, and the guns were in unprotected mounts and unready to fire, so attempting to man and prepare them would have been suicidal. The *Pueblo* got a radio message to the US Navy Security Group at Kamiseya, Japan, and they maintained radio contact until the North Koreans boarded the US ship.

The USS *Pueblo* communications techs used axes to smash equipment and began burning the classified documents and manuals. The North Koreans ceased firing and ordered the *Pueblo* to follow her into port.

The USS *Pueblo* followed at one-third speed as the crew threw equipment overboard. Then the *Pueblo* stopped, and the North Koreans opened fire again, killing crew member DC3 Duane Daniel Hodges* and injuring four other crewmen who were throwing materials overboard. The USS *Pueblo* resumed following at one-third speed.

The North Koreans ordered the USS *Pueblo* to stop and then a boarding party boarded the US Navy ship and captured her crew. The North Koreans immediately started beating the crew members and blindfolded them. Then the invaders navigated the *Pueblo* into Wonsan. The imprisoned crew of the USS *Pueblo* suffered eleven months of brutal torture at the hands of the North Koreans. They were finally released on December 23, 1968.

Why did North Korean Dictator Kim Il Sung order the capture of the USS *Pueblo* from international waters and hold the crew captive for nearly a year of savagery? What did he have to gain? And what part did the Soviet Union play in the incident?

Most popularly-accepted beliefs about North Korea's motives for hijacking the USS *Pueblo* and attacking South Korea's Blue House in 1968 were formed without the benefit of the vast quantities of Eastern Bloc diplomatic correspondence that are now available for review. These recently-available documents support new interpretations and challenge well-accepted views about the reasons behind the USS *Pueblo* incident.

When considering the US response, it's important to remember that in 1968, in addition to the US forces stationed in and near Korea, the US military equipped and maintained a costly military force with over three hundred thousand soldiers in Europe. The United States was also engaged in the expensive Vietnam "non-war" with the ground fighting at its most intense, including the ferocious battle of Khe San and the Tet Offensive.

The US Navy Seventh Fleet's first reaction to the attack on the USS *Pueblo* was to move warships closer to North Korea. Simultaneously, the Seventh Fleet staff planned for various responses ranging from a helicopter assault accompanied by carrier-based air support and fire support from destroyers and a cruiser, to plans for interdicting and capturing a North Korean freighter in retaliation. Also, during the first few weeks, more Pacific Fleet ships reinforced the Seventh Fleet, and the US Air Force ("USAF") moved more combat aircraft to South Korea and northern Japan.

The US Navy Pacific Command, the Pentagon, and the White House all agreed that any rescue attempt would likely result in the immediate murder of the USS *Pueblo* crew so no rescue was attempted. Also, after the CIA and Naval Intelligence informed the Pentagon that the North Korean merchant fleet consisted of seven small, low value freighters, the idea of a retaliatory seizure lost its appeal.

The White House formed a committee that included such lofty personages as Chairman of the Joint Chiefs of Staff General Wheeler, CIA Director Richard Helms, and Secretary of Defense Robert McNamara to manage the crisis and formulate an effective response. The majority of the American public was furious, but the Committee had to take into account that neither President Johnson nor the Joint Chiefs of Staff wanted a major escalation of the long-smoldering conflict in Korea. The committee reviewed a wide range of military responses from air strikes against North Korean Air Force bases to mining of North Korean harbors.

The Committee naturally gravitated toward plans that sought to damage North Korea's feeble economy with scenarios that did not involve major military strikes. However, after looking at the basic facts about the North Korean economy, the general consensus was that mining North Korean harbors would have little impact because the majority of North Korean trade was entering overland from the Soviet Union and the communist People's Republic of China. In general, economic targets in North Korea seemed less than spectacular because the economy there was in such a shambles. In fact, in 1968, doing economic damage to North Korea would have been a bit like rushing to punch someone before they could complete their own suicide. There just wasn't going to be much satisfaction involved in it, and it wasn't likely to impact the thinking, or chronic lack of thinking, by the North Korean government.

Some members of the US Congress felt that a strong response was needed and that the North Koreans should be threatened with a nuclear strike if they did not promptly return the USS *Pueblo* and her crew. Fortunately, President Johnson and the leaders in both Houses got everyone in Congress to focus on their shared priority—the safe return of the remainder of the USS *Pueblo* crew.

The United States attempted diplomatic contact via the Soviet Union, but at first the Soviets responded coldly. The North Koreans themselves lacked the expertise to extract much value from what they had captured, and they happily turned it over to the Soviet Union. The Soviets were busy extracting everything they could from the intelligence windfall that the *Pueblo's* secret coding equipment had provided them.

On the surface, it might appear that the Soviets were thrilled about North Korea's hijacking of the USS *Pueblo*. In fact, they were not as happy as most Western observers assumed they were in 1968. The Soviet Union, PRC, and the rest of the Communist Bloc did their best to maintain an appearance of solidarity to their own citizens and to the Western world, but divisions within the Bloc were far more severe than most Western analysts knew at the time.

Due to the Kim Il Sung government's inability to actually perform the usual basic functions of government, North Korea's day-to-day survival depended on the charity of Communist China and the Soviet Union. Communist China was, itself, suffering from the bloody and economically disastrous consequences of Mao's "cultural revolution," but in 1967 it had sent $150 million in military aid to North Korea, in addition to food and other commodities.

The figure seemed small to Western observers, but expenses incurred in helping the North Vietnamese burdened the PRC. Millions of people in the PRC were facing starvation. From 1958 to 1961, approximately twenty-eight million communist Chinese starved as a result of the PRC's misguided agricultural reforms. China's agricultural output had still not substantially recovered from the severe self-inflicted damage, so what might have seemed like modest aid to Western observers actually represented a significant sacrifice on the part of the PRC.

The Soviet Union also delivered significantly more aid to North Korea, via direct aid and one-sided trade agreements that benefited North Korea. On the surface, relations between North Korea and the Soviet Union seemed warm in 1968, but below the surface, Moscow was growing tired of Kim, and many Soviet leaders were regretting that the Soviet Union had not selected a better and more manageable puppet in North Korea.

By the late 1950s, the PRC was challenging the Soviet model for international communism, and the Chinese wanted to assume a leadership role over existing and potential communist states in Asia. As for the Soviets, they saw the Chinese as people to be tolerated and flattered as fraternal brothers in communism for the sake of the greater communist good. The Soviets believed they were the only ones qualified to manage world communism, and they expected other communist nations and communist movements to respect their position of supreme authority. When the PRC made it clear that it was not only not under Soviet control but was, in fact, attempting to lead its own communist bloc, the rift between China and the Soviet Union became a great chasm.

North Korean Dictator Kim Il Sung's response to the Chinese/Soviet rift was to try to maximize aid from both the PRC and the Soviet Union by pretending to be squarely in both of their camps simultaneously. In retrospect, we now know that from the point of view of the Soviet Union, Kim was seen as an aggravating and troublesome friend and a complete liability to the Soviet agenda. What Mao's assessment of Kim was remains more difficult to determine, but it appears that the PRC viewed him as a problematic puppet to manage. Both the Soviet Union and China wanted North Korea in their own camps, and both wanted Korea unified as a communist nation. However, both the Soviets and the Chinese were beginning to wonder if the usual "fraternal" struggle in the Korean peninsula was worth the cost.

It's probable that for Kim, the hijacking of the USS *Pueblo* had little to do with his view of the United States or his relations with South Korea and the West. He likely had more interest in creating an illusion of legitimacy for himself as a great, or at least believable, communist leader and player in the world communist struggle. He had every reason to assume that either the PRC or the Soviet Union or both were running out of reasons to continue supporting North Korea. If North Korea did not seem to be in danger of attack from the West, then there was less reason for those countries to continue to pump money into an irredeemable North Korean system.

In the great poker game of international communism, Kim only had one card to play, and that was the "I oppose the United States and the West" card. Beyond that, he wasn't in the game and could have easily been replaced at the table by a less ridiculous and more compliant North Korean. While to outsiders the kidnap of the USS *Pueblo* appears to be lacking in rationale and devoid of any positive potential results for North Korea, in existential terms, hijacking the *Pueblo* and holding her crew gave Kim Il

Sung both a reason to be alive and a method by which to remain alive within the international communist community.

Kim never understood the PRC's ongoing economic crisis or the limits of Soviet military might. With the help of his trained parrots in generals' uniforms, he convinced himself that if he could start another fight with South Korea and the United States, the PRC and the Soviet Union would pour massive amounts of military and financial aid into North Korea. Kim likely started to believe some of his own propaganda, along with that generated by the governments of other communist nations. He dreamed that the next Korean War would result in him ruling over a unified Korea, and he believed that his dream was reality.

While these twisted motives were difficult to see from outside of North Korea in 1968, the growing mountain of available declassified documents from the collapsed Soviet Union and Eastern European Communist Bloc concerning both the Blue House attack on South Korean President Park Chung-hee and the *Pueblo* incident now indicate gross miscalculations on the part of Kim. They also make it quite obvious that the Soviet Union and East Bloc nations viewed North Korea's hijacking of the USS *Pueblo* as inconvenient to their own foreign policy agendas.

When neither the PRC nor the Soviet Union increased military or financial aid to North Korea in response to Kim's urgent "call to arms," Kim at some point must have realized that he had gotten it wrong. After months of increasingly blunt diplomatic pressure from his fraternal communist pals, Kim agreed to release the crew of the USS *Pueblo* in exchange for a statement from the United States saying it was spying on North Korea and promising to not spy on North Korea again.

The United States was no longer particularly concerned with the ship, itself, beyond its propaganda value because the Soviets had long since extracted all of the information that they could from the equipment and documents. Once the crew returned on December 23, 1968, the United States considered the crisis to be over. As a result, as soon as the crew was safely out of North Korea, the United States repudiated the statement.

The US Navy convened a board of inquiry into the USS *Pueblo* incident. Although Captain Bucher and his entire crew had obeyed all orders and done their best to follow all prescribed procedures, the Board strangely recommended that Captain Bucher and the Pueblo's Security Operations Group Commander Lt. Steve Harris face courts martial. Wisely, Navy Secretary John Chafee rejected the Board's recommendation with the reason that the officers had already suffered enough.

While that was certainly true, Chafee was perhaps more motivated by the fact that the courts martial would have exposed the poor planning by the Pentagon and the NSA, along with the unworkable, indefinite, and divided command structure to which the USS *Pueblo* and all NSA-controlled US Navy ships reported. The fact that the *Pueblo* was allowed to operate 15 miles from the coast of North Korea in 1968 without proper protection from possible North Korean attack indicates an unworkable chain of command. Ships under clear Seventh Fleet control would not have been forced into in a similar situation.

During preparation for her mission, the USS *Pueblo* reported to the US Navy, but it received mission directives from the NSA and the White House via the Joint Chiefs of Staff, as well as by other informal and undefined channels of command. Lots of folks with no naval training were apparently in charge of directing the *Pueblo*, but no one in those multiple command chains seemed to be responsible for her safety or well-being. That was a formula for disaster.

The NSA documents concerning the USS *Pueblo* are informative and paint a picture of an inadequate understanding of naval operations on the part of the NSA. However, they are redacted, and only a small portion of the relevant records have thus far been released.

The issues of chain of command might have never been cleared up, but signals intelligence operations were evolving quickly, and the need for surface ship missions close to the shores of hostile nations was rapidly declining. Newer technologies in satellites and spy planes, along with the increasing capabilities of nuclear submarines, were revolutionizing signals intelligence gathering operations. Interestingly, the USAF would soon face similar issues of divided command concerning their ever-more-sophisticated reconnaissance and signals intelligence planes, but those are stories for another day.

North Korea has never returned the USS *Pueblo* to the United States so the vessel has never been decommissioned. It now serves as a tourist attraction in North Korea. It also remains one of many reasons why the United States and the West have no trust or respect for the government of the North Korean Kim Dynasty.

---

*DC3 Duane Daniel Hodges received a Silver Star. Marine Sergeant Robert Hammond received the Navy Cross for defending his fellow crew members at great risk and injury to himself by antagonizing the North Koreans to distract them from torturing the other crew members.

INTELLIGENCE FAILURES

———

OPERATION BARBAROSSA

Hitler and a Most Important Intelligence Lesson

The Soviet View

How Mussolini's Ego Saved the Soviet Union

———

AMERICAN CIVIL WAR

Paved with Bad Intelligence
The Road to Antietam

The South's Greatest Miscalculation

———

WORST INTELLIGENCE FAILURE IN US HISTORY

Response to Operation Drumbeat

15

WHY INTELLIGENCE FAILS?

PROSTITUTION MAY BE THE OLDEST PROFESSION, BUT SPYING IS THE second oldest. While no one knows when the first intelligence operative conveyed information to their government, historians can safely agree that spying dates as far back as the Iron Age. With such a long history, there are bound to be some fantastic successes and some dismal failures.

Considering past intelligence operations and their impacts can help us all to be better consumers of intelligence estimates. Taxpayers are the Intelligence Community's customers. In any democracy, the stated purpose of funding intelligence activities is to make us—the voters and taxpayers—safer and less burdened by the astronomical costs associated with national defense.

While considering cases of successful intelligence estimates can be useful, for two important reasons, we will instead take a look at some of the worst cases. First, we have a tendency to want to deal with the ugliest and dirtiest problems up front. A lifetime of living in the Great Hall of Mirrors tends to do that to old spooks like Holmes, and Piper is just bent that way. The greatest and ugliest problems are easiest to identify in the present, and, therefore, if we tackle them first, we can be certain that we are not throwing bundles of cash and human lives into a meaningless inferno of activity. This likely contributes to the "kill, cripple, or steal the biggest monsters first" mentality of much of the world's intelligence communities.

The second reason is personal. On the day Holmes decided to undertake these chapters, he was thinking about General Douglas MacArthur and his ineffective staff. Naturally, that left Holmes pondering horrible intelligence estimates.

Let us first consider some limitations inherent to any conversations on intelligence history. As of the time of publication, we are still learning more from previously classified or buried information that goes as far back as WWI. For example, Holmes spent five hours the other day barely scratching at the surface of newly released materials about US intelligence estimates in the 1960s. Another factor to consider is that a great deal of misinformation is often intentionally left in files to build a security wall between any researcher and certain classified information.

Also, old spies lie. They do it well, and worse yet, they do it neatly and effectively in concert with each other. In fact, on some level, most spies with field experience were paid by the taxpayers of their respective nations to learn to lie convincingly. While spies may not be liars in their personal lives, they lie to protect others who were involved in past intelligence operations and to protect any creative tradecraft they might have employed. Though the practice is necessary for security, it is admittedly unfortunate for historians.

Not that *Holmes* would ever be a spy himself. Spying is a disgusting activity that is conducted by loathsome creatures. He and his cohorts are nothing like that. They are nice people, and they have simply done a bit of necessary intelligence work against dangerous enemies—the aforementioned loathsome creatures. To be fair, we should mention that the loathsome creatures often take the opposite view as to who is loathsome, and who is a patriot. But then again, they are loathsome, so why would you take *their* word for it anyway?

Spying is almost always a controversial issue, so let's start with the case of a culprit that nearly everyone can despise. . . . No, not the political candidate that you didn't vote for. . . . Let's start with a German that few modern Germans would defend, Adolf Hitler.

16
HITLER AND A MOST IMPORTANT INTELLIGENCE LESSON

As THE NAZI DICTATOR OF GERMANY, HITLER INHERITED AN efficient and effective intelligence apparatus that was run by the German military establishment. So why did he then make so many crucial errors based on bad intelligence estimates? The answer is one of the most important lessons for managing intelligence efforts in democratic nations. Let us consider two of Hitler's many asinine mistakes during WWII.

Hitler had already committed some glaring errors based on faulty intelligence estimates by the time he ordered the invasion of Poland, but with the invasion, he attained new heights of miscalculation. In secret, he made the Molotov-Ribbentrop Pact with his archenemy, Joseph Stalin, for the partition of Poland, and Hitler did it without the advice of his military leaders, his intelligence service, or his best diplomats. It is difficult to imagine that Hitler had any good diplomats, but he did. Unfortunately, the German Foreign Office had been taken over by a pathological low life named Joachim von Ribbentrop. Ribbentrop was a dedicated Nazi and had no regard for logic or reason. He was also capable of tremendous self-delusion.

One result of Ribbentrop's colossal stupidity was that the many well-educated, dedicated, and intelligent employees of the German Foreign Ministry no longer mattered. Their assessments that invading Poland would likely force France, Belgium, and England into war with Germany fell on deaf ears.

Hitler found himself fighting the war he had not planned—a general war on his Western front. Then Germany's easy conquest of a numerically superior but unprepared Western Europe encouraged Hitler's increasing faith in his own propaganda. He became more convinced that he alone had a clear vision of the geopolitical realities of Europe. Rather than admit that his own military wisdom was inferior to that of the entire German military establishment's, Hitler became less willing to listen to his best generals and admirals. This led him to his next great miscalculation, Operation Barbarossa.

With much of her army spread across the globe, the United Kingdom was decimated on the fields of France, but her air force and navy were still largely intact. At the same time, the British Army, with material support from the United States, was rapidly rebuilding and expanding. With the United Kingdom and the United States growing closer, the German military was forced to maintain large garrisons of troops in the occupied countries from Poland to France.

Responsibility for controlling those nations was made more difficult by Hitler's infamous Waffen-Schutzstaffel ("SS") divisions and his secret police, the Gestapo.

While consuming military equipment and other resources, the barbaric SS and its ruthless Gestapo counterparts inspired loathing for Germany in the occupied nations. This made it impossible for the United Kingdom to seriously consider any peace agreement with Germany, and it made the German Army's massive occupation duties much more expensive in equipment and manpower. In those circumstances, no reasonable man would have invaded the numerically superior, wealthier nation of the Soviet Union. Unfortunately for all concerned, Hitler was nothing like a reasonable man.

Hitler's military intelligence apparatus and his General Staff accurately assessed that while Germany's well-trained and well-equipped army could take advantage of Stalin's gross mismanagement of the Soviet Union, they could not completely defeat the Soviets while still in a conflict with the United Kingdom. Hitler ignored their well-reasoned intelligence assessments and instead led Germany to ruin, albeit after inflicting millions of casualties in the Soviet Union.

The great lesson to be learned from Hitler's invasion of Poland and from Operation Barbarossa is one that, unfortunately, not all leaders have learned.

The most accurate intelligence estimates are useless when decision makers ignore them.

However, Operation Barbarossa is also an example of when two fools met, as Stalin managed to commit some similar mistakes to Hitler's with similar costs. Now we will look at the operation from the Soviet point of view.

17

THE SOVIET VIEW OF OPERATION BARBAROSSA

THE SOVIET UNION'S REACTION TO HITLER'S INVASION PROVIDES US with one of history's most glaring examples of bad intelligence assessments. Intelligence professionals reading this book should be aware that we use the term "assessment" in the generic English sense rather than in the technical professional sense. All intelligence agencies have their own requirements and rules for what an "intelligence assessment" should look like. We are not following any of those requirements other than the ones that coincide with the researching and writing of history.

To understand the Soviet Union's failure to adequately prepare for the German invasion of June 22, 1941, it's important to consider the decision-making process of the Soviets. Josef Stalin was a dictator who only nominally reported to the Communist Party of the Soviet Union. In reality, the Communist Party lacked the will or practical authority to oppose any decisions taken by Stalin. By 1941, everyone in the Soviet Union understood that disagreeing with Stalin about anything was likely to lead to arrest, torture, and possibly execution. Not surprisingly, Stalin had grown accustomed to people agreeing with him. While he may have enjoyed his success in bending the entire Soviet Union to his will, it had an isolating effect that would prove disastrous.

Even though Hitler vastly underestimated the war fighting capability of the Soviets, he understood that the Soviet Union's military was much larger than the armies of Poland or France. Accordingly, he instructed the German military to move approximately 3.8 million troops into position to invade the Soviet Union. Some of those troops were not for employment in the spearheads of the invasion, and, therefore, did not need to be kept close to the Soviet borders. Still, even in the pre-satellite age, it was difficult to disguise German troop buildups.

So how did Stalin manage to ignore the massive German buildup leading to Operation Barbarossa?

There are various opinions about the details of how and why Stalin failed to anticipate a German invasion, but some aspects are nearly universally accepted. One might assume that the Soviet Narodnyy Komissariat Vnutrennikh Del ("NKVD"), the precursor to the KGB, and Soviet military intelligence forces were inadequate or perhaps nearly blind to all evidence. This was clearly not the case.

The Soviet leadership considered itself to be in a perpetual state of war with the rest of the world. From their point of view, the character and intensity of that war varied, but there was no such thing as real "peace" with Western nations. The Soviet State also operated on the assumption that it was, and always would be, in a state of war with a significant portion of its own citizens.

These two fundamental assumptions caused the Soviet Union to invest heavily in intelligence efforts. Both the NKVD and Soviet military intelligence accurately assessed that Hitler was planning an invasion. They had done an excellent job of penetrating Hitler's Foreign Office, intelligence services, military staffs, and industry. They were also receiving more than enough information from a variety of independent sources to be certain that Operation Barbarossa was imminent.

In addition to its direct sources in Germany, Stalin's intelligence community was aware of US and UK assessments of Hitler's intentions. When diplomats from the United States and the United Kingdom informed Stalin of German plans to invade the Soviet Union, Stalin had already heard this from his own spies in those countries. He assumed that all the warnings coming from the Western nations were part of a Western conspiracy to force him to launch a premature war with Hitler. Stalin preferred to let the West demolish itself, and he planned to step into a convenient power vacuum of a destroyed Western Europe.

Opinions vary about precisely how, in the face of so much corroborative information, Stalin failed to anticipate the German invasion. In one sense, he didn't. Just as Hitler understood that carving up Poland with the Soviets would in no way appease Stalin's long term goal of annihilating Western nations and governments, Stalin clearly understood that Germany would try to attack the Soviet Union in time. Stalin's basic reaction to that reality was to attempt to outsmart the Western nations.

From Stalin's point of view, the United Kingdom, France, and other Western enemies were as much a threat to the Soviet system and Soviet ambitions as was Germany. All Westerners were Stalin's enemies, and all of them needed to be accounted for in the Soviet geopolitical calculus of the day. In addition to considering the threat from his Western neighbors, Stalin also had to consider the very real threat of invasion by the Japanese military to the east. Japan had already conquered vast swaths of China, and it could not be completely ignored.

Stalin responded to the threats that surrounded him by using his vast NKVD resources to try to maneuver Western countries into war with themselves, and by counting on the Japanese to continue being strategically diverted with their slaughter of the Chinese. From Stalin's point of view, Hitler's invasion of his Western neighbors fit perfectly into his plans.

Stalin never doubted that Hitler would invade, but since Germany was still busy dealing with the undefeated United Kingdom, Stalin was certain that Hitler would not make the mistake of throwing Germany into the same sort of two-front war that brought that country to ruin in 1918. When Stalin's intelligence services explained to him that Hitler was not going to wait for the fall of the United Kingdom to invade the Soviet Union, Stalin's megalomaniacal personality enabled him to ignore them. When anyone in his intelligence, diplomatic, or military organizations foolishly attempted to argue the point with him, he accused them of being enemy agents and had them murdered or banished to labor camps.

Since June 22, 1941, Stalin's miserable intelligence assessment of German intentions has been a popular topic of study. As more files have been obtained from the now-defunct Soviet Union, more explanations are offered as to precisely how Stalin managed to deceive himself. Thus far, the various theories and occasional new evidence have not changed the essential facts of the case.

Stalin failed to prepare for Operation Barbarossa because he refused to acknowledge that anyone might understand the strategic situation as well as or better than he could. The results of his grand miscalculation were devastating for the Soviet Union. We cannot assume that the best possible preparations by the Soviet Union would have completely and bloodlessly defeated the German invasion, but it is reasonable to assume that the Soviets would have suffered far fewer casualties in halting the German advances.

There is one other "what if" that we usually ignore when examining Stalin's grotesque mismanagement of the Soviet military machine. If, indeed, Stalin had been able to defeat Hitler's invasion more efficiently, then Soviet forces likely would have advanced further west before the Allied Forces reached the same positions. Then, the post-war division of European nations might have left even more European nations enslaved by Soviet occupation.

Stalin's horrendous failure to anticipate Operation Barbarossa reinforces the lesson that even the best intelligence is only useful when leaders use it effectively. Stalin's failure in 1941 also demonstrates another important lesson from intelligence history.

Nations and their leaders should be aware that their own plans and ambitions can blind them to their enemies' intentions.

In our next chapter, we will consider an oft-ignored intelligence wild card in Operation Barbarossa—Italy.

18

HOW MUSSOLINI'S EGO SAVED THE SOVIET UNION

IN THE FALL OF 1936, ITALIAN DICTATOR BENITO MUSSOLINI AND German Dictator Adolf Hitler announced a military treaty between their respective nations. From the beginning of this alliance, Hitler was convinced that Italy, a junior partner, could at best be most useful in countering British naval power in the Mediterranean and possibly in threatening the United Kingdom's hold on the Suez Canal. From Mussolini's point of view, the alliance with Nazi Germany entitled Italy to be treated as an equal partner. Mussolini expected the alliance to offer Italy opportunities to develop a Mediterranean empire that would stretch across northwest Africa and westward from Italy across the Adriatic.

In March of 1938, without any prior consultation with its Italian ally, Germany entered Austria and managed a coup that is remembered as "bloodless." The annexation of Austria was not actually bloodless, but Austrian resistance collapsed quickly, and Nazi propaganda efforts were somewhat successful in convincing the world that Germany was welcomed by the Austrian people. Mussolini was stunned both because Hitler had succeeded so easily in Austria and because Hitler had not consulted or even forewarned him of the invasion.

Later that year on September 29, France, Italy, the United Kingdom, and Germany signed the now-infamous Munich Agreement, which granted the Western portion of Czechoslovakia to Germany. While in this case Mussolini *was* consulted, his role was limited to helping bolster the feeble notion that the Munich Agreement was legitimate in spite of the fact that the Czechs were not consulted at all about how their country would be carved up.

In March of 1939, Hitler again surprised Mussolini by granting independence to the Slovakian areas of Czechoslovakia and annexing the remaining portion of that country. By this point, Mussolini was beginning to understand that Hitler had no intention of treating him as an equal partner in their alliance. Mussolini felt that he had to do something to improve his prestige, so without consulting Germany, Italy invaded Albania in the following month.

Albania had a poorly-trained and minimally-equipped army of 15,000 men. It was further impeded by the fact that it was already in a state of political turmoil due to tensions between communist, royalist, and democratic nationalist factions. The 100,000 Italian invaders managed a rare Italian victory, installed a puppet government, and declared that Albania was now part of Italy.

Hitler saw the Italian annexation of Albania as being a sensible move and was likely informed in advance by his intelligence agencies. From Germany's point of view, having Italy in control of the entrance to the Adriatic Sea from the Mediterranean supported Germany's long-term strategy for the coming war.

In August of 1939, again without consulting his Italian ally, Hitler signed the Molotov-Ribbentrop Pact, a non-aggression pact with the Soviet Union. Mussolini was angry and embarrassed at having been left out. He likely would have been far angrier if he had known that the pact included a secret agreement for a post-war division of Eastern Europe between Germany and the Soviet Union.

The following month, Germany and the Soviet Union invaded and divided Poland. France and the United Kingdom then declared war against Germany. In April of 1940, Hitler once again went on the warpath and unleashed his army on Denmark and Norway. Denmark fell in a day, and Norway managed to resist until June.

Hitler was quite pleased with himself, while Mussolini was feeling more and more like Hitler's weaker little brother. Mussolini decided he had to do something to prove that Italy was a modern military powerhouse. He confided to his generals, "To sit at the peace table, you have to make war." This was his way of voicing concern about post-war division of spoils between Germany and Italy after what he expected would be a quick war.

Mussolini made his "big move" in September of 1940. He attacked British-occupied Egypt—*after* prior consultation with Hitler. Unfortunately for Mussolini and Italy, things did not go quite as they expected. The British in Egypt were badly outnumbered both in men and aircraft, but their planes, tanks, and equipment were vastly superior to those of the Italians. The Italian attack on Egypt, which should have been a quick success for Italy, turned into an embarrassing failure.

Having achieved no success in the first month in North Africa, Mussolini did a huge favor for the Soviet Union in October of 1940. He invaded Greece. Mussolini was certain of a rapid victory over the smaller Greek Army. The Greeks were not convinced. The Italian invasion turned into an Italian retreat, and the Italians were in danger of being forced out of Albania by the Greek Army and Greek partisans.

Hitler was taken completely by surprise. He and his General Staff were focused on preparing Operation Barbarossa to invade the Soviet Union, and they had not informed their ally Italy of their intentions. As we point out in the previous chapter, Stalin was unconvinced of a German invasion. Mussolini also suspected nothing. Even when Germany moved massive amounts of men, equipment, and supplies to Poland, the Italian diplomatic and intelligence communities managed to miss what should have been obvious to them. This ignorance of Germany's planned invasion of the Soviet Union was instrumental to Mussolini's decision to invade Greece. It was an intelligence failure that sank Mussolini's military into dire trouble.

Hitler was furious. He refused to see that he had helped Mussolini stumble into this terrible mistake by not informing him of Operation Barbarossa. Italy plunged headfirst into an ill-timed operation in Greece instead of concentrating on the far more crucial campaign in North Africa.

In February of 1941, Hitler had to send German divisions and aircraft to help Italy in Egypt. By the time Germany was able to send adequate reinforcements to North Africa, the United Kingdom had also reinforced Egypt. In spite of the best efforts of Hitler's Field Marshal Erwin Rommel, his German Africa Corps, and three full corps of Italian troops, Rommel never reached the Suez Canal.* When compared to the immense scale of operations on the Eastern Front, the Axis defeat in North Africa might seem less important, but the failed North Africa campaign denied the Germans the use of several of their best divisions for their Soviet Union invasion, along with considerable resources of the over-taxed German Luftwaffe.

Hitler considered leaving the Italians to suffer their growing disaster in Greece on their own. However, as the Italian debacle dragged on towards the spring of 1941, Hitler decided that he had to save his Italian ally from complete defeat – not because Italy was his ally, but because Greece was no longer neutral and was now accepting aid from the United Kingdom. This meant that Greece had to be defeated, because if the British Royal Air Force was allowed to operate air bases in Greece, its bombers would be within range of the oilfields of Romania. Without Romanian oil, the German Army would grind to a halt in the Soviet Union.

In April of 1941, Germany and Bulgaria invaded Greece. By early June, Greece was defeated. So, all's well that ends well? No. It ended well for Germany, but it ended too late.

By June, the German Army should have been halfway to Moscow with trucks of supplies following it on mostly-dry, passable roads. The Russian road network was primitive, and the Germans could not afford to have their army's logistics further strangled by nearly impassable muddy roads. However, by the time Germany launched Operation Barbarossa, it was two months behind schedule, thanks to Mussolini's decision to invade Greece. Germany was also without valuable troops and equipment that now had to occupy the previously-neutral Greece. Before the German Army got close to Moscow and Stalingrad, supply problems on bad roads limited its armored operations. When the Germans finally did get to the gates of Moscow, snow was falling and the German Army was without winter clothing and equipment.

In the end, the vastly numerically superior Soviet Army and Soviet production defeated Hitler on the Eastern Front. However, if Operation Barbarossa had started on time, Stalin might have lost Moscow, Leningrad, and Stalingrad. If that had happened, Stalin could conceivably have decided to conclude a peace treaty with Germany, in which case, an early departure from the Soviet Union would have been disastrous for the Western Allies. Between Hitler's and Stalin's egomaniacal disregard for their own intelligence personnel and Mussolini's egomaniacal disregard for intelligence, Operation Barbarossa failed.

No nation should take for granted their ally's intentions. Even friends need to watch each other.

---

*See *Key Figures in Espionage*, "Hekmet Fahmy—The Fox Behind the Desert Fox," for more information on Rommel's espionage efforts in Egypt.

19

THE ROAD TO ANTIETAM

September 17, 1862, is remembered by US military history students as the bloodiest day in US history. It should also be remembered as a critical lesson to all members of the US Intelligence Community and the US military in how even a perfect intelligence windfall can be defeated by habitual bad intelligence.

On December 20, 1860, the South Carolina state government voted to secede from the Union, beginning the American Civil War with a bloodless political act. Many Southern politicians guessed that their states, too, could happily secede and slip away from the Union without suffering much loss. Wealthy Southern plantation owners thought that by seceding, they could continue to use slavery as their primary economic tool. Most Southerners did not own slaves or plantations, so the secession concept was marketed to them under the banner of "States' Rights." By May 1861, eleven Southern states had voted to secede and had formed the Confederate States of America.

President Lincoln, like a majority of Northerners, was opposed to slavery, but he thought that he was not in a position to declare an end to the practice. Slavery was still legal in the Union border states of Missouri, Kentucky, Maryland, and Delaware, and Lincoln did not want those four states to secede and join the Confederacy.

On May 24, 1861, the US government signaled its determination to reverse the secession of the Southern states by sending an army across the Potomac River. With the capture of Alexandria, Virginia, the US Army improved the security of nearby Washington, DC, and it established a valuable base for operations against the Confederacy.

For the Confederacy, it was critical to prevent a Union capture of its capital, Richmond, Virginia, and the surrounding area, including the agriculturally-rich Shenandoah Valley. When the Union Army moved south from Alexandria in July of 1861, the Confederacy concentrated all the forces it could muster for a counterattack. On July 21 at Manassas Junction, the Confederates soundly defeated an overconfident and unorganized Union Army and sent it into retreat to Alexandria. The battle is commonly referred to as the Battle of Bull Run.

The Union defeat at Manassas shocked the overconfident Northerners. For the general public in the South, the victory proved the superiority of Southern military abilities and indicated certain victory and independence for the Confederate States. Also, the Confederacy was hoping for foreign assistance from cotton-consuming countries such as France and England and from neighboring Mexico, and the victory at Manassas helped the South's diplomatic efforts.

While the general public in the South celebrated the victory at Manassas, most of the South's senior military leaders were not quite so willing to underestimate the North's military abilities or political determination to retake the Confederacy. With each passing month, more Confederate leaders realized that time was not on their side, and that the Union would eventually organize sufficiently to use its vastly superior resources in manpower and industry to win the war.

The Confederate leadership thought that their best strategy was to keep the Union busy on as many fronts as possible in order to ward off a major Union invasion of the South. They reasoned that, if the Confederacy lasted long enough, it would eventually receive enough foreign assistance to ensure its long-term independence. However, the single greatest diplomatic obstacle for the South in receiving foreign assistance was that it was seeking recognition and aid from nations that had already outlawed slavery. Those nations took a dim view of slavery in the Confederacy.

By the summer of 1862, the South's need for foreign aid was becoming more urgent. Confederate General Robert E. Lee thought that defensive victories on Southern ground would never be enough to gain the image of legitimacy that the Confederacy needed to acquire that aid. With the agreement of Confederate President Jefferson Davis and his cabinet, Lee devised a plan to invade Union territory in Maryland and West Virginia. They hoped that Maryland would respond to a Confederate invasion by joining the Confederacy, bringing much-needed conscripts and material wealth.

On September 2, 1862, Lee's Army of the Confederacy marched happily into Maryland. They might have been less cheerful if they had known that Lee's plans were based on an abysmal intelligence assessment of the conditions in that state. Although most Marylanders did not actively oppose Lee's army, they did not lend assistance or join his forces. The "liberation" of Maryland was not going as planned.

President Lincoln recognized Lee's invasion as a serious problem, but he also recognized a great opportunity. The Union's Army of the Potomac now had 75,000 well-equipped soldiers. That army was well trained by its popular commander, General George McClellan. McClellan loved that army, and that army loved him. Morale was high, and the troops were ready and willing to face Lee's soldiers.

While Lee moved his army forward on a foundation of faulty intelligence, the Union forces had their own intelligence issues. In 1862, there was nothing like a CIA, or even a fledgling OSS. McClellan relied on Alan Pinkerton and his informal intelligence service, and Pinkerton and his people spied efficiently.

However, although Pinkerton's men were able to gain access to Confederate information, Pinkerton lacked any basic ability to reasonably assess that information. He repeatedly overestimated the size of Lee's forces. President Lincoln and the Union War Department never believed Pinkerton's information, but McClellan did, and he operated accordingly. When McClellan maneuvered his army to oppose Lee, he did so under the assumption that he was facing a Confederate army numbering over 100,000 troops, when, in fact, Lee had 54,000. And so it was that two well-trained armies, both equipped with terribly inaccurate intelligence estimates, marched to battle.

Lee knew that McClellan was highly intelligent and skilled, as well as cautious by nature. Lee was also still hoping to inspire an uprising against the Union in Maryland, and he operated with the assumption that he could defeat McClellan by maneuvering more quickly than the Union Army. Then, for uncertain reasons, Lee violated a major rule of warfare. He divided his forces in the face of a superior enemy and sent Stonewall Jackson's troops to capture weapons and supplies at Harper's Ferry.

On the morning of September 13, 1862, Union troops of the 27th Indiana Infantry rested in a meadow outside of Frederick, Maryland. They serendipitously took their break at a site that had previously been the location of General Lee's headquarters. At that site, Sergeant John Bloss and Corporal Barton Mitchell found a piece of paper wrapped around three cigars. Known as Lee's "Lost Orders," the paper was a message containing Lee's detailed plan of battle, addressed to Confederate General D.H. Hill. The men promptly delivered it to their commander.

The Indiana Division's adjutant general, Samuel Pittman, recognized the handwriting in the message as belonging to his pre-war friend Robert Chilton, now the adjutant general to Robert E. Lee. Pittman delivered the message straightaway to General McClellan. McClellan boasted that with the information he now had, he would gladly be willing to go home if he could not defeat Lee. This boast was, in fact, a hedged bet. If, with the intelligence windfall he had in hand, he could not produce a resounding victory, he should have gone somewhere less pleasant than "home."

The new information wiped out Pinkerton's terrible intelligence assessment. McClellan now knew that Lee's army was dangerously divided into five sections, and that it stretched out over a 35-mile area split by the Potomac River. McClellan was 12 miles from the nearest Confederate unit at South Mountain. He was in a position that all commanders dream of in their wildest drunken moments. In their sober moments, they never dare to hope for such generosity from the capricious gods of war.

McClellan, poised to become the great Napoleon-like general that he always knew he could be, did what Napoleon never would have done. He waited. Then he waited some more. His division commanders grew restless. Then they grew anguished. Elation fermented into quiet disgust. Finally, after eighteen hours, McClellan gave the order to move.

By now, much of Lee's army was concentrated in favorable high ground near Antietam Creek. Lee had used the time granted him to send forces to plug the pass at South Mountain. His troops had set up defensive positions there and slowed McClellan's advance.

The Union Army finally approached Lee's Confederate Army on September 16. Stonewall Jackson's troops had still not returned from Harper's Ferry to Lee's position. Lee had less than 40,000 men, and their backs were to the Potomac. McClellan's 75,000 well-rested troops could have conducted a successful flanking maneuver against the Confederates. If McClellan had fallen off his horse or gotten drunk, they likely would have. Instead, McClellan allowed his uncertainty about the intelligence to confuse a clear and reasonable battle plan. McClellan delayed the attack until the following morning.

On the morning of September 17, Union Army General Joseph Hooker led the assault against the now well-entrenched Confederate forces. Rather than concentrating a reasonable portion of his forces against a single point of the Confederate line, McClellan allowed the battle plan to devolve into consecutive piecemeal attacks.

Confederate General Jackson and his troops finally arrived in time for Jackson to earn the nickname "Stonewall" for his defense of the Confederate flank. By the end of the day, both armies had suffered terrible casualties. The dead, wounded, or missing numbered 12,000 on the Union side and 10,000 on the Confederate side. It was the bloodiest day in US history at that point in the war.

The balance of losses left McClellan with an even greater numerical advantage in that a larger percentage of his army was still capable of battle. Over 25,000 of his army were fresh troops that had not yet been engaged. Lee, on the other hand, had no fresh troops remaining. The Confederate lines had held, but they were overall in worse condition than the Union troops. McClellan could still have captured or killed Lee and his army.

With victory staring him in the face, rather than pressing his advantage, McClellan agreed to a truce for both sides to recover their wounded and bury their dead. When night fell, Lee thanked God and withdrew from the field as quickly and quietly as he and his army could. He salvaged enough of his forces to return to defend Virginia, preventing McClellan from having a straight shot through to Richmond. George McClellan had squandered a golden opportunity to deal a crippling blow to the Confederacy.

Lincoln was disappointed in McClellan's performance, but, unlike McClellan, he knew how to seize an opportunity. The victory at Antietam Creek gave him public relations momentum, and on September 22, 1862, Lincoln announced his Emancipation Proclamation.

The Proclamation would not take effect until January 1, 1863, and even then it was conditional. Only slaves in Confederate territory were freed. Slaves in the four Union slave states still remained in bondage. In other words, the Emancipation Proclamation was the Civil War equivalent of today's Canada making a proclamation that only applies to the United States and not to any territories in Canada.

Since the Confederate States were not inclined to obey any Union proclamations any more than the United States is today inclined to obey any proclamations from Canada, only around 40,000 slaves in captured Confederate territory were actually freed at the time of the Proclamation. However, the real impact of the battle was that Lincoln was able to score a monumental diplomatic victory. After the victory at Antietam and the Emancipation Proclamation, no European nation was willing to *openly* support the Confederacy in a war to defend the institution of slavery.

Due to poor intelligence and the mishandling of intelligence, Lee miscalculated the sentiments of Maryland, and McClellan dawdled away a windfall opportunity. Lee allowed himself to anticipate a states' rights event in Maryland and to believe that men would throw themselves in for the Confederates, and he launched a campaign that he had little chance of winning. McClellan refused to accept and act on the best intelligence, and he dawdled away the chance to crush Lee's army and march on Richmond. Nearly three more years of bloody war remained to be fought, but the fate of the Confederacy was sealed.

It was a case of a perfect intelligence windfall being defeated by the habitual misuse of intelligence.

As US General George Patton often said, "A good battle plan now is better than a perfect battle plan tomorrow. Intelligence windfalls such as the one McClellan received are rare gems. They can turn the tide of war, but only if acted on promptly. When you get time-sensitive intelligence, don't sit on it.

20

THE SOUTH'S GREAT
MISCALCULATION

ON A PLEASANT SPRING DAY ON APRIL 12, 1861, AMIDST A CARNIVAL atmosphere with stylish picnicking revelers, Confederate General Pierre Gustave Toutant-Beauregard ordered his artillery to open fire on Union-occupied Fort Sumter in the Charleston harbor in South Carolina. A merry time was had by all except for Union Colonel Anderson and the men trapped in the fort. After thirty-four hours of bombardment, Anderson was allowed to withdraw his men by way of a Union Navy ship, and in exchange for safe passage, the remains of the fort were surrendered to the Confederate States of America. Beauregard was hailed as a Caesar by the jubilant picnickers and by their cousins across the Confederacy. Four hellish years and 630,000 dead Americans later, the festive spring day had become a five-star hurricane disaster.

The official stated aim of the Confederacy was to maintain "states' rights" against the threat of federal intrusion by the administration of the new president, Abraham Lincoln. Although not all Southerners were willing to claim the defense of slavery in the South as their cause for secession, it was the one federal intrusion on states' rights that concerned them, in spite of the

fact that Lincoln had made it clear that his priority was not aboli-
tion, but preservation of the Union. Politics and cultural sensitivi-
ties aside, Alabama, Arkansas, Florida, Georgia, Louisiana,
Mississippi, North Carolina, Tennessee, Texas, South Carolina,
and Virginia seceded from the Union to form the Confederate
States of America in order to maintain the institution of slavery
and to allow their individual states to operate with less central
authority from any national government.

By May of 1865, the Civil War had brought about two major
changes to the US federal government. The first was the growth
of the authority of the federal government and the correlating
drastic decrease in states' rights. The second change was that
slavery had been abolished in the Confederate States by that
same now-more-powerful federal government. States no longer
had the right to individually decide the issue of slavery.

When, after a century and a half of deliberation and debate, we
view the South's fatal choice to undertake a civil war with the
United States, any student of military or political history has to
wonder how the Southern leaders managed to make such a bad
decision. What could Beauregard and his political supporters
have expected when they opened fire on Fort Sumter? Clearly,
they expected a surrender of the undersupplied and undermanned fort. In this they were correct, but what did they think
would follow? We cannot blame Confederate President Jefferson
Davis and other leaders in the Confederacy for lacking clairvoy-
ance, but there were well-known facts that should have enabled
them to draw a more accurate intelligence assessment on the
prospects of war with the Northern States. Let us consider some
important facts that were readily visible from the beginning.

The Union had the following:

- Twenty-three Northern states

- A free population of approximately 22,000,000 and over 450,000 slaves
- Jobs to offer immigrants
- Over 120,000 factories
- A well-established international banking system with over $100 million total in deposits
- Iron production in 1860 of 2,700 tons

The Confederate States of America had the following:

- Eleven Confederate states
- A free population of approximately 6,000,000 and close to 4,000,000 slaves
- Few jobs to offer immigrants
- Twenty thousand factories, many of which were small and close to the Mason-Dixon Line, making them vulnerable to military attack
- Few banks, with less than $38 million total in deposits
- Iron production in 1860 of only 155 tons

To add to the disparity, the Northern states had a canal system and 20,000 miles of railroads covering approximately 98 percent of Northern routes. They were almost completely on a standard gauge, and an engine in New York could, and did, run just as easily in Michigan. This consistency allowed tremendous capacity to transport passengers, cargo, and communications.

The South, on the other hand, had railroads, but no railroad system. An individual investor built in any fashion that he saw fit, and an engine in Virginia was not likely to be able to traverse the state of Virginia, much less operate in Mississippi. That lack of cooperative planning and central regulation haunted the South throughout the duration of the Confederacy and gave the North a decided advantage.

As a result, on the eve of the American Civil War, the North had the guns, the manufacturing capability, and the manpower. The South had cotton and four million slaves. When the odds are considered, it seems the North would have had a clear advantage; however, the South was counting on three factors not normally reported in censuses and almanacs.

First, it was counting on fighting a defensive war, with no need to invade the North. The Union Army would have to invade the South to recapture it and force its re-entry into the Union. As a general rule of warfare, the aggressor needs a three-to-one advantage over the defender. Given the weapons available in 1861, Southern military leadership was not unreasonable to consider being outnumbered two-and-a-half to one an even match. Those military leaders included over three hundred trained US Army officers who had resigned from the US Army and received commissions in the Army of the Confederate States of America. They were some of the best and most experienced military leaders in the United States, and they would not have encouraged secession from the Union if a secession would have required conquering Northern states.

Second, and more subtle, the Southern leaders calculated nearly correctly the unwillingness of "lazy city folks" in the North to enter military service and campaign in the South to free slaves that, in the South's estimation, most Northerners cared nothing about. There were always war protestors in the North during the Civil War. However, their influence was never enough to force Lincoln to prematurely halt the war, which was something the Southerners did not grasp in time.

The South's third ace up the sleeve was the 1861 equivalent of an OPEC oil embargo. The South knew, or thought they knew, that European nations would not tolerate an interruption in cotton trade. In weighing the odds for war, many Southern leaders were confident that Europe would threaten intervention and coerce the United States into accepting the Confederacy's independence. Guns, ammunition, and the massive mountains of manufactured goods required to feed the gluttonous gods of war would flow from Europe to the South like oxen to the sacrificial altar.

That being said, it was no surprise to the Confederacy that the United Kingdom was reluctant to send its navy to defeat the Union Navy blockades of Southern ports. Southerners knew that Queen Victoria considered slavery an abomination and was reluctant to defend the interests of wealthy slave owners in a fight against the United States. However, the South was accustomed to life in a democracy, and it was prepared to coax the British Parliament and the Queen into seeing the Southern light. The Confederacy played the "cotton card." It stopped exporting cotton to England.

What the South did not grasp was that the Brits had been at the trade game for a long time, and they were good at it. After all, a small island nation with mothers who aren't known for their cooking, artists who aren't known for their painting, and army officers who buy their commissions does not come to rule the waves by being stupid. The United Kingdom had seen that Southern move coming a mile away, and it was ready.

In 1860, a bumper crop of cotton glutted the markets. In anticipation of the South's move, the United Kingdom invested substantial long term capital in stockpiling that crop. Also, far from London, and even farther from the cotton fields of the South, British colonial officials in Bombay saw an opportunity in the chaos caused by the anticipated cotton embargo. The Bombay area had the perfect climate and soil for growing cotton. It also had something better than slaves. The United Kingdom had cheap, disposable workers who showed up willingly and worked for less than it cost to maintain an American slave. The

United Kingdom outsourced its need for the Southern slave labor to India, Egypt, and Africa.

Cotton production in those three regions grew quickly. By 1863, England had little concern for what happened to the mountains of cotton bales being stockpiled in the Confederacy. The United Kingdom no longer needed the South. The guns, ammunition, and gold were not forthcoming for the Confederacy from Europe except at high prices. Cotton was, in fact, not quite king after all. It was nothing more than a commodity.

The South, for lack of economic and political intelligence, discovered that its ace in the hole was only a jack, and that jack was a knave. It is true that the shortage of cotton imports from the Confederacy *did* hurt England for a time. However, the problem was only short-lived. Thousands of English laborers were laid off, but even after losing their textile jobs, the British working class remained strongly anti-slavery and pro-Union. As a result of those sentiments and the need for employment, thousands of those work-hungry Irish, English, and Germans immigrated to the Northern United States, where US Army recruiters promising citizenship and bonuses to enlistees were waiting at the docks. The North didn't have to count on its potatoes getting off of their couches to fight, because by 1863, many Union regiments had immigrant majorities in their ranks. The Southerners had almost correctly calculated that North would not be willing to pay the high price in blood that it would take to defeat the Confederacy. They did not anticipate the influx of immigrants or that the North would have so many new citizens to sacrifice to the cause.

If the South had collected and correctly analyzed information on the burgeoning cotton industry the British were fostering in India and Africa, its excellent military leaders would likely have reached a different conclusion about the wisdom of taking on the Union. Now, cotton, the plantation elites, and the American president who had to fight almost more against his Northern cohorts than against the Confederates are all gone. The great-great-grandsons of the slaves remain, and, although the reconstruction and social evolution have yet to be complete, the Union remains, as well.

Across the South and at Gettysburg, Pennsylvania, gravestones mark the resting places of silent witnesses to a war fomented in ignorance, in arrogance, and from a complete intelligence failure. While Jefferson Davis had been acutely aware of the many disadvantages faced by the Confederacy, he and his supporters allowed their passions to lead them to gross miscalculations.

As a result, the great intelligence lesson to be learned from the suicidal miscalculations of the Confederate States of America is one that is still relevant today.

Passions and emotions have no place in intelligence analysis, and romantic delusions will not win on the battlefield.

21

US RESPONSE TO OPERATION DRUMBEAT

IF YOU ASK HISTORIANS TO NAME THE WORST INTELLIGENCE FAILURE in US history, many will name the December 7, 1941 attack on Pearl Harbor. We will depart from that conventional wisdom. Pearl Harbor was, indeed, a major intelligence failure for both Japan and the United States, but, in and of itself, it was not the worst US intelligence failure during WWII. In our opinion, the more prolonged, costly, and agonizing disaster was the US failure to predict and counteract the onslaught of German U-boats against US merchant shipping in Germany's Operation Drumbeat.

For those who have already read the chapter on spy ships in WWI, don't bother flipping back to double check. You heard us correctly. The same United States that failed to embrace the threat of the German U-boats in WWI hit "instant replay" and failed to appreciate and prepare for the threat of the German U-boats in WWII.

Yes, we know. A reasonable person would think that the United States would have learned its lessons in WWI. This just illustrates a hard fact of warfare. There are few battles and few wars that are decisive for all time, and few lessons that are learned deeply enough to survive past a generation. Most victories and lessons are only secured for their own time and place, and they are not something our children and grandchildren can take for granted.

As in WWI, it was expensive to organize convoys, and merchant sailors and their shipping company bosses were still not accustomed to being under military control. Also, there was no legal authority in democratic nations to order convoying. Adding to the complexity of the problem was the fact that, since the successes of the U-boats in WWI, Lloyd's of London was no longer willing to insure UK shipping. The UK government took over that task, which meant that the financial burden of shipping losses fell on the UK taxpayers to bear.

As a result, when the United Kingdom entered WWII on September 3, 1939, there was no universal agreement on the necessity of convoys on either side of the Atlantic, even after the experience of WWI. Faced with the threat of the U-boats, and having no consensus on what to do about that threat, the United Kingdom began convoying ships on a small scale.

On September 5, 1939, US president Franklin Delano Roosevelt declared that the United States, which had not yet entered the war, would conduct "neutrality patrols" for the purpose of observing and reporting belligerent warship movement in a "neutrality zone" that extended for hundreds of miles off the coast of the Western Hemisphere. Part of the duties of the US Navy and US Coast Guard included escorting merchant vessels in trans-Atlantic voyages.

Officially, these escorts were not for the purpose of defending shipping to and from the United Kingdom, which included supplies and munitions from the United States. *Officially*, the patrols were to defend the United States's right to trade on the oceans. . . . That's right. Political spin was not invented in the twenty-first century.

It just so happens that the very first neutrality patrols began on September 6, 1939, just one day after President Roosevelt's announcement. This might lend anyone familiar with the "speed of government" to agree with Holmes's belief that Roosevelt already had an understanding with Chief of Naval Operations Admiral William D. Leahy on the matter. That the neutrality patrols were enacted so smoothly indicates the Navy had already announced them and sent out the orders privately on September 3, and more publicly on September 4th and 5th. However, these patrols for observation and limited convoying of trans-Atlantic merchant vessels were not enough to prevent the success of Germany's U-boats.

The German submariners literally referred to 1940 and 1941 as the "happy times." Though Germany only had thirty-nine submarines at the outbreak of the war, the Germans kept them busy.

Only thirty-nine? Yes. Hitler had told Germany's U-boat fleet commander, Admiral Karl Dönitz, to plan for war in 1944 or 1945. It came sooner. However, Dönitz was a man who knew how to make do with what he had, and the German U-boats were like a pack of wolves in a hen house. While they picked off the Allied merchant ships, Germany was ramping up production, and it would manufacture nearly one thousand submarines by the end of the war. Make a note of that number. We'll be discussing it again.

In spite of the German U-boat success, by the end of 1941, the equation was changing. The U-boats were still effective in sinking Allied merchant ships, but with increasing risks to themselves. Germany declared war on the United States on December 11, 1941 and enacted Operation Drumbeat—an operation in which most

German submarines were sent to the US Atlantic coast specifically to destroy merchant shipping and to inflict as much damage
as possible.

At this point in the war, Allied trans-Atlantic shipping had
largely been organized into convoys with inadequate, but significantly effective, naval escorts. The UK's Royal Navy and, to a
lesser degree, the US Navy, US Coast Guard, and Canadian
Navy ships primarily provided these escorts—the Canadian
Navy because Canada was at war with Germany, and the US
Navy and Coast Guard because of the neutrality patrols.
Though these escorts were undermanned and poorly-equipped,
they made it more difficult and far riskier for German
submarines to conduct effective attacks against the merchant
vessels. However, there were *still* no convoys in US coastal
waters.

Attacks on US coastal shipping began on January 12, 1942, 300
miles east of Cape Cod. In the first seven months of 1942, German
submarines, aided in small measure by Italian submarines, sank
609 Allied and neutral merchant ships in US coastal waters. Two
hundred thirty-three of those were US ships. And the Germans?
They lost only twenty-two U-boats during that period. Indeed, it
was the German submariners' second happy times of WWII.

It is astounding that the US government did not use its authority
to immediately order convoying for all coastal shipping and
blackouts for all coastal lighting as soon as the country entered
the war. Germany, though delighted, was also astounded at the
lack of credible US response. The losses of merchant seamen and
shipping tonnage piled up. Finally, FDR agreed to order convoys
and blackouts in the summer of 1942. They were phased in by the
end of August. Once these simple measures were instituted, the
monthly losses of merchant sailors and shipping began to
decline, and German submarine losses increased.

We feel strongly that it is important to calculate the death toll of the merchant sailors, even though it is impossible to do so with accuracy. Holmes's best estimate is that nearly six thousand died in those 609 sinkings. Along with them, thousands of tons of weapons and ammunition, millions of barrels of oil, and precious food supplies desperately needed by the British were lost.

We apologize to family members of the merchant marine sailors that served so courageously during WWII for our inability to accurately state their losses. Several factors prevent an exact count. The first confounding factor is that there was no central registry for merchant sailors at sea. Each shipping company kept its own records, and many did so poorly. Sailors were often added to a crew immediately prior to sailing and were not always counted in the casualty lists. Second, many of the sailors survived the sinkings but later died of their wounds. A third factor that had been ignored until recent years is the fact that the Allies made a concerted effort to understate shipping losses in order to not damage the public's morale. The losses were appalling, and, sadly, they were greater than they needed to be.

Some might point to the fact that the US Navy and Coast Guard did not have enough ships for all of the convoys. The Navy needed the budget and the steel for aircraft carriers, battleships, and cruisers. However, it was still a political failure in that we did not put more resources into coastal waterway protection in the early months of 1942. As few as a dozen more Hamilton class cutters would have made a critical difference in protecting merchant vessels along our shores and likely would have saved thousands of lives.

By the time Operation Drumbeat came to bear in January of 1942, the United States and her allies had a clear understanding of what had occurred during the first year and a half of U-Boat attacks against allied shipping. Thanks to the brilliant efforts of men like Captain Frederic John "Johnnie" Walker RN, Captain Donald Macintyre RN, and Captain John Waters USCG, the Allies were developing more effective methods of combating German submarines. They accomplished this tactics such as Captain Walker's Creeping Attack and with several new weapons, like the Royal Navy's Hedgehog system. Sonar systems, radar systems, and radio detection triangulation systems also improved by the month to result in a reduction of Allied losses.

Given all that had occurred in the North Atlantic by January 1942, the US response to Operation Drumbeat seems unforgivable, and there are few intelligence failures in US history that can compare with it. It is true that the US Navy and US Coast Guard were limited in the ships and planes that they could employ against Operation Drumbeat, but those that were available were poorly employed. While the United States was not in a position to use all the readily-available intelligence to formulate a completely effective response to Operation Drumbeat, better and more timely efforts would have resulted in far fewer dead merchant sailors and much less loss of ships and critical cargoes.

Even when a perfect response is not available, the best possible preparations must be pursued in a timely fashion.

THE COLD WAR ERA

———

Flight of the Konkordski

Overflights and Posturing
U2 Incident and the Cold War Dance

Eyes in the Sky

When China Spanked Vietnam

Bringing Down the Cosa Nostra

That Damned Berlin Wall

Vladimir Putin
Living Legacy of the KGB

22

LIFE IN THE COLD

FROM THE END OF WWII IN 1945 UNTIL THE FALL OF THE UNION OF Soviet Socialist Republics government in Russia in 1991, Western nations faced off with the Soviet Union, its allies, and its captive satellite states in what became known as the "Cold War." Basically, the Soviet Union, led by the ruthless Joseph Stalin, perceived that it was its duty to spread communism throughout the world. For their part, Western nations governed by democracies were committed to keeping the entire world from falling under Soviet domination.

In the term Cold War, the word "cold" comes from the notion that neither side wanted the war to escalate to open warfare, and the "war" reference accurately describes the basic intentions of each side toward the other. It was first coined by George Orwell in his 1945 essay, *You and the Atom Bomb.*

From 1945 until August of 1949, the United States and the United Kingdom had a monopoly on atomic weapons and could have easily pushed the Soviet Union out of Eastern Europe. For a variety of reasons, the Allies declined to do so. Once the Soviet

Union acquired atomic weapons in 1949, avoiding war with the Soviet Union became a priority for the West.

Both East and West sought to harm each other and defend themselves with methods short of all-out war. One method employed in the conflict was the constant attempt by both sides to bring neutral or unaligned nations into their respective camps by means of diplomacy, bribery, economic incentive, armed coup d'état, or coercion. Another method employed was aggressive espionage and, at times, armed covert action.

The United Kingdom and France had been active in espionage against the Soviet Union since its birth in 1918. For its part, the Soviets, under the auspices of international communism, had been actively spying on the United Kingdom, France, and all European nations since before WWI.

Although the United States would become the preeminent contestant in the Cold War, prior to WWII, the United States felt comfortable relying on an isolationist strategy and didn't see a need for an intelligence service beyond whatever minimal activities the State Department might be involved in. Even during WWI, the US efforts in espionage were minimal.

The Soviet Union viewed the United Kingdom as "the main enemy" prior to 1946, and the United Kingdom remained the priority target for Soviet espionage efforts. However, long before the United States bothered to conduct espionage against the Soviet Union, the Soviets had hundreds of agents in the United States.

Most Western citizens think of the Cold War as being without casualties, except during the proxy wars in Korea and Vietnam. Few Westerners will even remember that the Allied nations fought a war against Soviet-backed communists in Greece from 1946 -1949, or that the United Kingdom struggled with a communist guerrilla war in Malaysia until 1960. Beyond the publicly acknowledged battlefields in Korea, South East Asia, Lebanon, Grenada, and Panama, the United States thus far acknowledges 382 American servicemen killed in combat against communist forces between 1945 and 1991. This figure does not include the officially-acknowledged civilian losses of the Central Intelligence Agency and other civilian personnel, nor does it include the deaths of "denied" personnel working under deep cover.

We believe the figure of 382 to be wildly low, and a long, smoldering debate is currently underway in Department of Defense and CIA circles concerning Cold War casualty figures. It is unclear how casualties should be counted and how much information should be released.

After a lifetime of living in a necessary state of denial, old hands have well-founded fears about releasing too much information. For one thing, releasing dates and locations of deaths will assist belligerent parties in identifying and killing those who assisted US efforts. Our word was given that our friends would never be exposed, and they never should be.

For nearly four decades, the deaths of American Cold War combatants were explained away as accidents and sudden acute illnesses. Wives and mothers buried their husbands, sons, and daughters without ever knowing what happened. The battlefield deaths of most of America's Cold War combatants will likely remain unrecognized for years to come in order to protect the living. Someday, if a future generation gets around to dealing with the information, it will likely seem too distant for anyone to pay much attention to it. This is a natural consequence of the type of battles fought.

If it seems sad, we should remember that it is far less sad than the alternatives would have been. Armageddon was avoided. Freedom was not lost. That matters, at least to us, and to those who have gone before us. Holmes and his brothers and sisters in the clandestine services paid a price. He knew none who were unwilling to pay that price quietly. None can now regain their lives by being identified.

When we review espionage activities from the Cold War, it is easy to take an academic view. If the seriousness of some of the participants seems almost comical from our current perspective, they seemed far less humorous at the time that they occurred. The events seem distant now. The causes may have been forgotten by many and never understood by some. We point out the issue of casualties in an attempt to describe an important aspect of clandestine activities during the Cold War—the contestants on all sides played for keeps.

Between the bright lights of international diplomacy and the dark cloud of the threat of nuclear war, life in the shadows in between was a bit different. Holmes and others feel as though they have lived in a parallel world far away from this one. They walked through this world every day, careful not to leave too many footprints here on their way to somewhere else. That other world became their home. This world, where we trust our neighbors and love our children, is the world that they desperately wanted to see remain intact. But in a sense, Holmes and his clandestine brothers and sisters will always be visitors here in this world that we hold so dear. For some of them, their home remains somewhere else, far away.

23

FLIGHT OF THE KONKORDSKI

ON JUNE 3, 1973 IN PARIS, OVER TWO HUNDRED THOUSAND
spectators at the Paris Air Show watched the new British/French
Concorde supersonic transport ("SST") perform a fly by followed
by a fast, steep climb. A new age of Mach 2 passenger flights was
supposedly dawning in the skies above Paris.

Among the spectators was an anxious Russian. While watching
the Concorde, Alexei Tupolev waited for the pass of one of the
most important aircraft in Soviet history. The loud roar of the
approaching Tupolev-144 ("TU-144"), dubbed the "Konkordski"
by Western media pundits, must have been a comfort to him.

The TU-144 represented more than an aircraft for the Soviet
Union. Over a decade of research, politics, espionage, and coun-
terespionage had gone into the design and test work that
produced the TU-144. The Paris air show was a chance for the
Tupolev design team to bring an advanced commercial airliner to
Western markets and lay the groundwork for sales to the West.

Those sales would bring desperately-needed Western currency to
the Soviet state banking system. The acceptance of the TU-144 by

Western markets and media would represent a coming of age for Soviet industry in the ruthless open markets of the West, and Moscow desperately needed the influx of foreign currencies and the boost to reputation of the Soviets' technical prowess.

For the great Russian engineer Andrei Nikolayevich Tupolev and his son Alexei, the TU-144 was the product of years of long hours at the factory, pushing forward an ambitious project that must have been near and dear to both of their hearts. Andrei and Alexei had to know that without cash sales to airlines outside of the Soviet Union, no amount of great design work could push the Soviet SST project further into the future. They would be out of funding. The Kremlin would not be willing to support the massive project simply for the few planes that Aeroflot could purchase. Only Andrei's reputation as a genius engineer and a loyal hero of the Soviet Union had convinced Soviet leaders to risk the immense investment in the development of the TU-144 transport. Unfortunately, Andrei Tupolev died six months before the Paris Air Show.

The TU-144, piloted by Mikhail Kozlov and Valery Molchanov, flew the routine pass by the airshow crowd and proceeded to begin a maneuver that was designed to outdo the performance of the Concorde. In the final hours prior to the airshow flight, Soviet engineers made last minute modifications to the flight control systems to allow the TU-144 to make an impressive turning climb. This last minute equipment modification indicates that the Soviets knew hours in advance of the show what maneuvers its competitor, the Concorde, would make.

Although they expected a minimum five-mile air space to be maintained empty for their flight, Kozlov and Molchanov were not alone in the air over Paris that day. Besides the other four members of the aircrew, they shared the air space with a French

Mirage fighter. The Mirage had been tasked with flying close above the TU-144 to obtain mid-air photos of its forward canard wings.

After making an impressive starboard turn, the TU-144 appeared to be on approach for landing when it suddenly started into a steep climb. The plane canted, and apparently one of the canard wings could not handle the force. It detached. Some theorized that the detached canard wing punctured a wing tank. The TU-144 burst into flames before hurtling to the ground, killing the pilot, the six-man air crew, and eight French civilians on the ground.

But how did the possible stall, or even the loss of a canard wing, cause the explosion? The fireball was about the size one would expect for a downed aircraft, but the shock wave reached further. Before the story ends, and at the time of publication it hasn't quite ended yet, the shock waves reached London, Moscow, DC, Seattle, and lots of back alleys at points in between.

The French military was responsible for the accident investigation, and, at least outwardly, they maintained a cooperative stance with the Soviet Union. They even entertained requests to fly some of the wreckage to the Soviet Union.

At first, the French government claimed that there had been no Mirage fighter near the TU-144. We can hardly imagine that none of the 200,000+ spectators at the show happened to notice the Mirage—or possibly pair of Mirages—flying by the TU-144.

So why did such an important plane on such an important day, flown by some of the Soviet Union's best air crewmen, self-destruct? What happened?

Several answers have been offered. As Holmes's wise father would say, "Where you stand depends on where you sit." Before deciding where to sit, we would do well to consider a bit of the history that led the Concorde, the TU-144, and the Mirage to Paris on that spring day.

Andrei Tupolev sat at a design table. He had been sitting there since graduating engineering school in 1918. If you have never liked a Russian and you feel guilty about it, here's your big chance to remedy that.

On November 10, 1888, Andrei Nikolayevich Tupolev was born near the Volga River in the village of Pustomazovo in the Tver Governate of the Russian Empire. Tupolev was an early communist or communist sympathizer, and while in college, and he was arrested in 1911 because of it. He was released in 1914 and allowed to return to school. After graduating in 1918, Russia's leading aviation engineers quickly recognized him as a remarkable talent.

Aviation was still in its infancy, and Tupolev was highly influential in its survival and development inside of the young Soviet Union. One might assume that his early Communist Party work prior to and during the Soviet revolution would have placed this exceptional engineer above the suspicion of the police state. Don't be silly. On October 21, 1937, the minions of Stalin's self-destructive Soviet police state visited the Central Aviation Institute and promptly arrested the entire staff, including Andrei Tupolev. Why? Blame it on German engineers.

The Soviets had ignored the advice of Tupolev and his fellow visionaries at the design bureau. As a result, the Soviet aircraft were failing miserably in the Spanish Civil War when piloted by young, poorly-trained volunteers against the German aircraft flown by Franco's Nationalist Air Force and members of Nazi Germany's Condor Legion.

Stalin and his cohorts had plenty of intelligence on the Luftwaffe, and they hadn't needed to go far to get it. In violation of the

Treaty of Versailles, the Soviets secretly allowed the Nazis to operate a military pilot training facility in Lipetsk, Russia, starting in 1924. The Soviet Union had watched Germany build its pilot cadre for the Luftwaffe from a grandstand seat.

Stalin's sycophants had miscalculated—miscalculating was their finest skill—and they assured their Idiot in Chief Stalin that their Soviet aircraft would be victorious over the hated Germans in the Spanish Civil War. They weren't. Someone was to blame. Obviously, Stalin and his morons making the aircraft production decisions could not be at fault. Arrest Tupolev!

Most of Tupolev's coworkers were executed as saboteurs. He and the other survivors were moved to an NKVD work camp where they went back to designing airplanes, but with less to eat and no warm place to sleep. Tupolev was run through a quick sham trial and convicted of sabotage. He was sentenced to ten years in prison and kept at the "aviation science prison" that the Soviet police state had so thoughtfully created for him and his fellow literates.

In 1944, after seven years in prison, Stalin ordered Tupolev released for "important work." The important work had to do with the Allied aircraft that at times landed inside the Soviet Union. Periodically, British and American planes returning from long bombing raids against Germany ran low on fuel and touched down on the Russian side of the line. When that happened, the Soviets impounded their aircraft or delayed their departure so that Tupolev and other top Soviet engineers might examine them. Also, when American aircraft flying missions against Japan in the Pacific theater ended up over Soviet lines, the Soviets simply impounded the craft. That was because the Soviet Union was not at war with the Japanese until April 13, 1945—after the United States, the United Kingdom, and their Pacific allies had defeated Japan.

In 1945, three USAF B-29 bombers landed in the Soviet Union after bombing Japan. The B-29 Flying Fortress was the most advanced heavy bomber yet produced, and Tupolev was ordered to create an exact copy of it for large scale production in the Soviet Union. He did. If you care to compare interior and exterior pictures of the US B-29 and the Soviet T-4, you will see that, except for a paint job, they are the same design. The T-4 was important to the Soviet Union because it gave the Soviets an aircraft capable of delivering the nuclear weapons that they were designing in preparation for the post-war standoff with their "Allies" that the Soviets were already planning.

After Stalin left for that big gulag in the sky, the new Soviet boss, Nikita Khrushchev, denounced Stalin's many purges as a terror. He "reformed" Tupolev and developed a friendship with him. Apparently, both Andrei and Nikita enjoyed bantering unashamedly, using the most vulgar language in front of anyone who heard their conversations.

In 1956, Tupolev's TU-104 jet transport entered service with Aeroflot. It was only the second Soviet jet transport to enter service. Under Khruschev, Tupolev became an icon of the Soviet state. He was the poor village boy who suffered for the revolution, survived Stalin, and went on to prosper as a great engineer—a most human hero that Soviet workers found relatable. It played well.

After Leonid Brezhnev led a successful plot to remove Khrushchev from power in 1964, Andrei Tupolev declined in popularity. His projects became more difficult to fund as compared to projects from other design bureaus, such as Ilyushan. Tupolev remained productive even without the patronage of Khrushchev, but his struggles to acquire funding became monumental. Then, on December 23, 1972, Andrei Tupolev died in Moscow after a long illness. His son Alexei, the

TU-144's lead designer, was left highly invested in the success of the aircraft.

France and the United Kingdom were less enthusiastic about the development of the TU-144. The United States was ambivalent toward both the French/UK Concorde and the TU-144. So where did the Americans sit on June 3, 1973? We will need to glance at a bit of American history to answer that question.

In the 1940s and 1950s, aviation was evolving rapidly. Once USAF Colonel Chuck Yeager broke the sound barrier on October 14, 1947 in a Bell X-1 rocket plane, engineers raised their expectations for aircraft capabilities. Most of the design efforts in the United States, Europe, and the Soviet Union were directed toward newer and faster fighter and bomber designs.

Passenger flight was expanding at the same time, too, as airlines hungered for more efficient, more reliable transport planes. Naturally, dreams of SSTs began to solidify into planning and design work.

In the United States, Boeing, Curtis-Wright, Lockheed, and North American all set their sights on a Mach 2 airliner. They and the Federal Aviation Administration estimated that eventually a maximum market for five hundred aircraft would grow and justify the cost of the development and production. By the 1960s, the US aircraft industry had extensive experience in supersonic military aircraft, and that experience helped the rapid pace of the design competition. Great designs began to emerge.

In 1966, Boeing and Lockheed each presented exciting, high-performance designs to the federal government. Both designs were funded, but before they went into production, economics and the taxpayers intervened. Ranchers in the remote areas of the United States were willing to tolerate sonic booms generated by USAF and US Navy military training flights, and most rural

Westerners were willing to shrug it off as "the sound of freedom." Urban dwellers, on the other hand, were not quite as forgiving. As talk of multiple daily supersonic flights became more popular, the public expressed concerns about the noise generated by supersonic flights. The market for domestic SSTs in the United States began to dry up before it ever came to fruition. That drastically changed the economics of the SST projects.

Lockheed and Boeing both developed designs for SSTs capable of Mach 2.8 cruising speeds, as compared to the Mach 2.2 speed of the Concorde. They also both found themselves looking at an ugly bottom line. The expense of producing and fueling the aircraft would have generated passenger ticket costs that too few passengers could afford. Between public resistance to sonic boom and ozone damage concerns, along with dismal economic projections, both projects lost steam. In 1971, the US government stopped funding them.

Before the Concorde and the Konkordski took to the skies above Paris, the United States dropped out of the SST market, both as consumers and producers. The race field was comfortably narrowed, but the market had also dwindled. By the time of the Paris Air Show, there was little margin for error for either the Concorde or the Konkordski.

With the United States out of the SST competition due to costs and increased political resistance, the French/British team felt confident that they would be able to corner the market for SST aircraft for at least ten years. The French and British were vaguely aware that the Soviet Union was developing an SST, but they were certain that the Soviets were two to three years behind the Concorde development project.

In 1963, a British delegation led by UK Aviation Minister Julian Avery had visited the Soviet Union and was given a limited tour of Russia's aviation industry. One of the things the Soviets showed the delegation was a model of the future TU-144. Avery and his team decided that the model looked like an all-out copy of what was then the early version of the Concorde design. When Avery returned to the United Kingdom, he warned the French and British that they obviously had been penetrated by spies.

This begs a question. Why would the warning even be required? Would the French and British not have assumed that the Concorde project was a target for the Soviets? Soviet KGB agent Sergei Pavlov was ostensibly the head of the Aeroflot's French operations, but he was, in fact, in charge of Soviet espionage for aviation in France. The French Intelligence Service placed Pavlov under more extensive and skillful surveillance after the delegation's visit.

Before long, Pavlov was observed collecting tire samples from a French airport employee. The French and British decided that, rather than arrest Pavlov, they would turn, or "double," his French contact and feed him bad information. The degree to which the planted bad information impacted the Tu-144 project can probably be accurately estimated by the British and French intelligence services, but if they have done so they are not yet talking publicly about it. In 1965, the French arrested and deported Pavlov, taking from him a complete copy of the blueprints for the Concorde landing gear.

While the obvious assumption is that the Soviet Union spied on the Concorde in order to copy the design work, the Soviets' actual goals were a bit more complex. Tupolev was under enormous pressure from the Soviet government to move quickly and to conduct a successful test flight before the Concorde did. The Tupolev firm had become famous for being able to put up a working aircraft for testing and early production and then later refining out the problems that had been missed or ignored in development.

To Western engineers, this might seem like a risky strategy, but Andrei and Alexei Tupolev lived in a different world. The political climate in the Soviet Union in the late 1960s was marked by much of the same urgency and desperation that had defined the Soviet Union during WWII. For Tupolev, beating the Concorde was more important than refining the best design. The Tu-144 needed to be flown as soon as possible, and the design could be finished later for a production run.

In the summer of 1968, the Soviets received intelligence that the Concorde would undergo its first test flight in early 1969. The Tupolev design team went into overdrive. Engineers and technicians were housed at the assembly area and worked with little sleep. In December of 1968, the TU-144 flew a successful test flight. The Soviets had been able to fly the first Mach 2 airliner in history.

The Kremlin was overjoyed. Andrei Tupolev and the lead engineer, his son, Alexei, had achieved a great dream. Andrei's expertise at redesigning hastily-produced aircraft would undoubtedly help get the Tupolev "fixed" prior to production, but in the meantime, they had struck a blow for the reputation of the Soviet Union. When a few months later the Concorde made its first test flight, some of the publicity value had been lost to the TU-144's earlier flight, but the test pilots of the Concorde had a more finished product.

By the time of the 1973 Paris Air Show, the British and French likely felt more than the usual Cold War hostility to the TU-144 project. If the Soviet espionage showed in the general design of the Tupolev-144, the British and French anger about the aircraft was just as obvious.

The Concorde team was warned that a Mirage III would be in the air, waiting to intercept the TU-144 to photograph the deployed canards in flight. Naturally, the TU-144 crew was not told of the

Mirage III. Also, the Tu-144 had its exhibition time cut in half at the last moment. Now, the TU-144 team would be flying a suddenly shortened flight plan with a control system that had been modified the night before.

At a reception the previous evening, Russian pilot Mikhail Kozlov had made it clear that he intended to push the envelope the next day, and that he would out-fly the Concorde no matter what. At the last minute, Soviet copilot Valery Molchanov agreed to carry on board a French TV crew's camera and film the cockpit during the exhibition flight. It seemed like a great opportunity to further the PR mission of the TU-144. The variables for creating an accident were quickly stacking high.

Here is what Holmes suspects happened:

When the Mirage III came into position to photograph the canards of the TU-144, the pilot, Kozlov, was either startled into an evasive maneuver, or, for purposes of an impressive show, simply pushed the envelope further than the airplane could go. Both possibilities are accepted by people who know much more about flight than Holmes does. Both possibilities lead to the same result.

During the abrupt maneuver, the air pressure to the engines dropped off, and some or all of the four engines stalled. The rapid change in velocity of the aircraft may have caused the heavy TV camera to strike the flight controls, complicating the pilots' attempts to save the plane. The pilot forced the TU-144 downward in order to gain airspeed with which to restart his engines. He only had 4000 feet of altitude with which to work, and after getting some or all of the engines running, he attempted to pull out. The abrupt climb exceeded the structural limits of the TU-144, and she broke apart.

The explosion before hitting the ground was not unusual. The TU-144 was fueled with volatile JP-6 fuel. There would have been plenty of heat in the disintegrating wing root and the engine compartment to ignite the vapor that formed from the fuel being released into the fast-moving air. Fuel + Oxygen Pressure + Heat = Fire. The more you have of any one of these factors, the less you need of the other two. The oxygen pressure was high, and the fuel vapor was close to ideal so the ambient air temperature, itself, might have provided enough heat for ignition. No other bomb was needed.

The accident investigation report never mentioned the Mirage III. The black box flight data recorder was supposedly never recovered. This strikes Holmes's non-aviation mind as comical. Two aviation engineers agree with him that the accident in question should not have vaporized the black box.

The French and Soviets seemed to cooperate in a cover up. So what was covered up? The Soviets wanted to blame the flight crew, as they were trying to sell a plane, not a crew. In Holmes's opinion, the French government did not want to be blamed by its French political opponents or the French public for the eight dead French civilians. The French and the Soviets, with UK acquiescence, made a deal and jointly accepted the most comfortable explanation for the accident.

In the aftermath, many theories surrounding the Paris Air Show incident, and the Tupolev Design and the Mirage III's impact on the accident have been interpreted differently by a variety of observers. It's often easy to know someone's political views by listening to their analysis of this and other events. Claims have even been made that the Mirage, or possibly two Mirages, purposely flew in front of the TU-144's intake, intentionally causing two of her engines to stall. However, the French could have taken down the TU-144 without instigating a crash over a populated area. Also, if the French were going to purposely cause a crash for the TU-144, they likely would have done it while the plane was en route to Paris rather than at the Air Show.

Many Russians and Soviet sympathizers hasten to point out that the TU-144 was different from the Concorde, and, therefore, was not a copy. It was, in fact, quite different. The TU-144 wing design was simpler than the Concorde's on the original Tu-144, but it was changed on later models. The braking system on the TU-144 was primitive compared to the Concorde's brakes. The hydraulic system in the TU-144 was completely unlike that of the Concorde, and the Concorde used a clever cooling system that the Tu-144 did not have. The exterior noise level of the TU-144 was lower than the Concorde's, but the noise in the passenger space was almost unbearable. All differences aside, the Russians' claim that the TU-144's earlier first flight proves it is not a copy is nonsensical, but it's the sort of thing that the average journalist or college freshman might believe. The TU-144 was not a copy of the Concorde, but the Tupolev design team benefitted from the Soviet espionage successes against the Concorde.

In 1977, four years after the TU-144 crash in Paris, Soviet agent Sergei Fabiew was arrested by the French intelligence services. He had been working without diplomatic cover and, therefore, was subject to prosecution and a likely long prison term. The French convinced him to cooperate.

Fabiew delivered cipher codes to the French that he should have destroyed long before his capture. He was obviously hedging his bets and had no desire to return to the Soviet Union. The French were able to use the old ciphers, along with cryptology information from the Americans and the British, in order to decipher old messages from Moscow to Fabiew. It was clear that Fabiew's claim of having provided the KGB with full sets of plans for the Concorde was not just boasting. He had gotten every bit of the

Concorde at every step of the way. From whom? And how could the French not know?

In 1973, the US Federal Aviation Administration banned supersonic transport over the United States—a ban still enforced at the time of publication. Occasionally, perhaps when the wine flowed freely at lunch, a few French writers and foreign journalists opined that the ban was out of jealousy for the Concorde, and, therefore, destroyed the future of the Concorde at its inception. No. The US aviation industry would have faced the same SST flight restrictions that economically stunted the development of the Concorde, so the United States didn't bother developing an SST of its own. Furthermore, the French had originally planned a continental version of the SST, and it was the British who insisted on a transatlantic-capable SST.

The Concorde went on to break the transatlantic speed record in 1999. That commercial flight record still stands. The Concorde was retired from service in 2003 after passenger demand dropped due to growing safety concerns, rapidly climbing maintenance costs, and escalating fuel costs which combined to make the plane unprofitable to operate.

And the Tu-144? It was quickly relegated to cargo duty due to cabin noise, inadequate cabin cooling issues, and Aeroflot's dislike for the plane's safety and maintenance concerns.

On May 12, 2001, Alexei Tupolev died. The Konkordski, stolen or not, lives on. In 1996, the US government funded a NASA project to operate the last TU-144 as a test bed for supersonic flight testing.

The espionage surrounding the Concorde was part of a much larger effort by both East and West to remain informed about their enemies' flight capabilities. Those efforts stretched around the globe from hangars in Seattle to banks in Macao and Switzerland and points in between, and they would require a voluminous book to describe *en totem*. If it seems outrageous that the Soviet Union spied on the Concorde project, we should remember that France, the United Kingdom, and the United States were all doing the same thing to the Soviets. The Soviet efforts against the Concorde were inconsequential compared to the spy ring they operated in Seattle and Portland against US aviation manufacturer, Boeing.

While the Concorde builders saw this as an earthshaking espionage case, as the Cold War went, this was really one of the cooler corners of that war. From the US perspective, this was a minor sideshow. To the Soviet politburo, it was important more for propaganda and commercial value than for flight development.

In late 2010, Russia quietly mentioned that it had, indeed, had the flight data recorder all along. The Russians said that, according to the analysis of the data, it was clear that pilot error was the cause of the accident, and that, based on radar trace data from the incident, the Mirage was not in position to startle pilot Mikhail Kozlov into taking evasive action. According to the current Russian explanation, the Tupolev team made a series of decisions that were individually reasonable, but when combined, they left the pilots flying a hastily-planned routine outside of previously tested parameters. According to the Russians, Kozlov pushed the envelope too far for the prevailing conditions and exceeded the structural capabilities of the TU-144.

Half a century after getting funding for the TU-144, the Tupolev firm sought funding from the Russian government for a liquid hydrogen/liquid oxygen fueled Mach 6 bomber that will enter space for Mach 20+ flight speeds and carry an eight ton payload. However, after two decades of Putin-led Russian kleptocracy, science and engineering initiatives have suffered significantly.

The Mach 6 bomber initiative, along with Russia's powerful new aircraft carrier fleets and many other Russian military dreams, remain, for now, Putin fantasies. If the Mach 6 bomber ever does comes to the Paris Air Show, we'll be sure to avoid Paris that week, but we bet if Andrei Tupolev were still alive, he might be up late trying to figure that one out. We'll see where it goes.

24

U2 INCIDENT AND THE COLD WAR DANCE

By Nigel Blackwell*

IN DECEMBER OF 1959, THE UNITED STATES, THE UNITED Kingdom, and France simultaneously proposed to Soviet Union First Secretary and Communist Party Chairman Nikita Khrushchev that they hold a meeting to "consider international questions of mutual concern." Khrushchev agreed, and the Paris Summit was arranged for May 16, 1960, in Paris. Among the topics of "mutual concern" was the Berlin situation, where the Soviet Union was furious that its citizens were escaping to the West, and a Test Ban Treaty, which would have slowed nuclear weapons development and perhaps prevented further proliferation.

Eisenhower, leary that the Soviet Union would under- or over-exaggerate its weapons stockpiles in any negotiations, approved the use of the U-2 spy plane to obtain photographic evidence of Soviet nuclear capabilities. The U-2 was born in the Cold War and designed to carry cameras at 70,000 feet, a height where the

United States believed its pilots would be safe from the enemy fighters and missiles of the day.

On April 9, 1960, Bob Ericson flew a U-2 from northern Pakistan across the southern half of the Soviet Union and landed in Iran. The Soviet Air Defense Force made several attempts to intercept him, but they were unable to reach his altitude. The photographs were valuable, and the CIA declared the mission a success. A second mission was planned.

A second CIA pilot, Francis Gary Powers, departed from the same northern Pakistan base on May 1, 1960, with a planned zigzag route north, overflying ICBM sites and plutonium production facilities, and landing at Bodo, Norway. Obviously, the route was planned to avoid known surface-to-air missile sites, since altitude was the U-2's only means of defense.

After Ericson's flight, the Soviet Air Defense Forces had been on red alert, and they scrambled to intercept Powers with an array of aircraft and ground-launched missiles. Some 1200 miles inside the Soviet Union, near Yekaterinburg, they did.

At the time, the United States only knew that Powers had appeared to descend rapidly from 65,000 feet to around 34,000 feet before disappearing from their radar. The USAF and the CIA assumed that Powers could not have survived the rapid descent, and the United States formulated its public statement based on that assumption.

The Soviet Union, on the other hand, knew that the aircraft had been brought down and the pilot picked up by a group of puzzled locals, who disarmed Powers and drove him to the authorities. In Powers's book, *Operation Overflight: A Memoir of the U-2 Incident*, he relays that he didn't even have a cover story planned, and as he was captured by a carload of locals, he realized practically everything he carried was carefully labeled "Made in the USA." He even carried a US flag.

Soviet leader Nikita Khrushchev announced that a US plane had crashed within the Soviet Union, and the United States immediately generated a cover story. NASA announced that it had lost a weather plane when its pilot reported he was having oxygen problems. They even painted a U-2 in NASA colors and distributed leaflets describing the "weather aircraft" to prove it was operating the U-2. Statements were issued to the effect that "there was absolutely no deliberate attempt to violate Soviet airspace and never has been."

Unfortunately, Nikita Khrushchev had a public relations ace up his sleeve when, a week later, he reported the following: "I must tell you a secret. When I made my first report, I deliberately did not say that the pilot was alive and well . . . . and now just look how many silly things they [the Americans] have said." In the remaining week before the Paris Summit, Khrushchev kept public pressure on the United States by staging the presentation of Gary Powers and the wreckage of the U-2. The United States back-pedaled on the NASA weather aircraft story, juggled to defuse the situation, and tried to establish access to Powers, all while preparing for the summit in Paris.

The Soviet Union was expected to use the U-2 incident to its advantage at the meeting, but no one knew how. Anticipation grew when Khrushchev arrived two days early. When Eisenhower arrived the following day, Khrushchev ignored him and visited French president, Charles de Gaulle, and British Prime Minister Macmillan. Khrushchev would later claim this was because Eisenhower hadn't indicated an interest in meeting, but neither de Gaulle nor Macmillan had done so, either.

In his own meeting with de Gaulle, Khrushchev presented a document outlining the Soviet Union's displeasure over the U-2 incident, along with three conditions for his participation in the Paris Summit, namely that Eisenhower should do the following:

1. Condemn the US Air Force's provocative act—which must have made someone in the CIA smile, because it was a CIA operation.
2. Guarantee that the United States would refrain from such acts in the future.
3. Punish the individuals responsible for the U-2 operation.

Eisenhower, de Gaulle, and Macmillan knew that should the contents of the Khrushchev document be leaked to the public, Khrushchev would have no way to back down without losing face. In fact, by presenting his demands to the British and French, it may have been Khrushchev's intention that they were leaked to the press. Either way, at the opening of the Paris Summit, where the four powers were to discuss the agenda items for the meeting proper, Khrushchev made public his demands.

Eisenhower stated that overflights had been suspended and would not be resumed, but on the other points, he was silent. Khrushchev postured and berated the United States for some time and eventually ended by withdrawing a long-standing invitation for Eisenhower to visit the Soviet Union. It was a public slap in the face for Eisenhower.

The meeting collapsed at this point. Khrushchev departed Paris. The Test Ban Treaty was stalled for three more years, and even then it was highly limited in scope. The situation in Berlin persisted, and citizens flowed out of East Berlin until the Soviets built the Berlin Wall to keep them in—a symbol of their failure.

The Soviet Union played the part of the grievously wounded for all they could and sentenced Powers to ten years in prison, only to release him within two years in exchange for a Soviet spy caught in the United States. The Soviet Union did no posturing on that occasion. Perhaps they found it hard to justify the difference between a spy at 70,000 feet and one on the ground.

The failure of the Paris Summit disappointed many around the world. Some say that Eisenhower could have handled the situation better. Some say that the United States should not have put so much at risk with the overflights. In the end, it is always possible that Khrushchev had already decided to walk away from the conference, and the downing of Gary Powers gave him the perfect excuse. We will never know.

---

*Nigel Blackwell was born in rural Oxfordshire in England. He has a love of books, a PhD in Physical Chemistry, and a black belt in pointing out the obvious. In a thirty-five-year career as an engineer, he has developed a wide variety of avionics for commercial and military aircraft, specializing in safety critical systems.

As a writer, Blackwell has collaborated with New York Times best-selling author Diane Capri on the bestselling Jess Kimball thriller series. Alone, he authored *Paris Love Match* – the story of an engineer who encounters the mob, a bag of diamonds, and a girl to die for . . . and finds out that's exactly what might happen if he doesn't think fast.

Nigel has driven trains, crashed single-seat race cars, and travelled much of the world. He now lives in Texas with his wife and daughter, where they enjoy the sunshine and listen to the coyotes howl at night.

25

EYES IN THE SKY—SPY PLANES

MUCH OF THE MOST IMPORTANT WORK IN ESPIONAGE WOULD NEVER play well in a Hollywood movie—no sports cars, no fancy parties, no gun fights, and no explosions. Most is just danger combined with dysentery from Third World mystery meats and boredom punctuated with an occasional win. It is important work done by those who will never get the glory, but who keep taking risks and doing the work anyway out of dedication to keeping our country safer. Some of those dedicated personnel are in ground operations, and some are the brave men and women who, even in this age of drones and other unmanned vehicles, still fly missions over "denied" airspace to glean intelligence we cannot gather any other way.

When we think about military aviation heroes, most of us think about the epic deeds of fighter pilots and bomber crews. While those pilots and crewmen deserve the recognition that they receive, there are thousands of pilots and air crewmen that have performed less glorious, but extremely dangerous missions. Most of them will remain forever unknown.

During the Cold War, from September 1945 until December 1991, the United States and her allies relied on a variety of intelligence and reconnaissance sources for information about the Soviet Union, the People's Republic of China, and their allies. Most of us are familiar with the basic idea of spies, or "HUMINT," as the Intelligence Community generally refers to human intelligence. It is also common knowledge that we keep satellites aloft for collecting visual, radar, infrared, communications, and electronic signal data over denied areas. Other publicly known sources for intelligence and reconnaissance are the once-secret SR-71 Blackbird, U-2 flights, and electronic surveillance stations. And though they are largely ignored in popular media, spy ships and other various ships play an important role in gathering intelligence, as well.

During the Cold War, more obscure, crucial intelligence programs conducted by the United States and its allies involved inconspicuous aircraft that flew hazardous missions along borders of the Soviet Union, North Korea, and Warsaw Pact countries. These Cold War Era missions gathered types of information that satellites and the higher-flying U-2 and SR-71 planes were unable to collect. These intelligence-gathering flights involved a wide variety of seemingly unremarkable aircraft packed with an assortment of photographic, infrared, and electronic monitoring equipment. While many of them were conducted in international airspace, some were assigned to enter enemy airspace. Because the missions were classified, as far as the friends and families of the flight crews ever knew, their loved ones were only involved in mundane weather reconnaissance, cargo flights, or training missions with various allies.

Lacking the altitude of a U-2 or the altitude and extreme speeds of an SR-71, these flights always avoided anything resembling a routine schedule or set flight areas. They often tried to take advantage of bad weather and nighttime to reduce their sitting duck status when crossing through denied airspace. The precautions helped, but they were far from a foolproof defense.

The exact number of aircraft that were shot down by enemy missiles and fighters will probably never be known. The flights were classified, and more than one authority conducted them. The CIA, the USAF, and the US Navy were all involved in assorted programs that sent crews into denied airspaces. In addition, US intelligence agencies at times contracted with civilian groups to run flights in denied air space. In some cases, US agencies even employed foreign contractors to conduct these missions. That lack of a single reporting agency or a single chain of command makes it difficult to accurately determine the number of aircraft that were downed by enemy defenses.

Lacking a clear, accurate number, Holmes estimates that approximately one hundred twenty spy planes were lost during the Cold War. The number of lives lost is unknown and difficult to calculate because missions in larger aircraft did not always carry the same number of air crewmen. Some of the aircraft shot down were small planes with just a single pilot on board. On the other end of the spectrum, some missions were flown in modified B-29 bombers ("RB-29s") converted for intelligence missions. The RB-29s were able to carry large cameras and other equipment, but they were neither quick nor stealthy. Those crews could have had as many as a few dozen people. What we know is that the US Cold War veterans groups have been able to tabulate 428 military and civilian air crewmen as dead or missing from spy plane missions. These numbers do not take into account missions flown by Allied aircrews.

One of the speedier and more common platforms for photoreconnaissance missions during the Cold War was the USAF's F-101 Voodoo. Unfortunately, small, fast planes like the Voodoo were limited in how much of a mission package they could carry. As a result, many missions involved large airliner-type aircraft converted for military use, such as the US Navy's P-3 Orion, which was based on the Lockheed Electra airliner.

In the post-Cold War Era, new strategies and new equipment are being developed and new aircraft are coming on line. One highly-capable USAF spy plane is the innocent-looking Northrup Grumman E-8. The E-8 Joint Surveillance and Target Attack Radar System ("J-STARS") aircraft provides long-range reconnaissance, targeting, and command and control capabilities to the US military, and it played a critical role in our wars in Iraq and in the Balkans in recent decades.

Development of a follow-up program to replace the J-STARS is currently stalled. Holmes speculates it's likely that a cheaper and more invincible unmanned aircraft is being developed to take its place. The new system will hopefully be better able to fly in the denied airspace of our peer and near-peer adversaries.

At the same time, the US Navy's venerable P-3 is being replaced by the new P-08. The P-08, based on the Boeing 737 airliner, is known to have powerful, highly classified maritime surveillance capabilities. In particular, it is excellent at locating submarines at sea.

As we develop new defense technologies, we must never forget that other players in the intelligence game are doing all they can to steal those advances. Communist China is at the forefront of those efforts. Given the rapidly increasing capabilities of the PRC Navy and PRC's expansionist imperial agenda in the Pacific region, the P-08 and its mission package are critical intelligence targets of the PRC government, and the Chinese have already made inroads into their acquisition.

In September of 2015, Lt. Cmdr. Edward C. Lin, a Taiwanese-born US Navy flight officer and P-08 crewmember with extensive training and experience in signals intelligence, was arrested on charges of espionage. Lin had also served as the Congressional Liaison for the Assistant Secretary of the Navy for Finance Management and Comptroller from 2012 to 2014. In his position as liaison to Congress, Lin would have had access to a vast array of sensitive information from every part of the US Navy. Lin's history as a congressional liaison and his access to the technical secrets of the P-08 made him a high-value target for the PRC and any other foreign government. Both communist China and Taiwan hit their mark.

Some details about the Lin case are obscure and others are classified. From what is public, we know that Lin told the US Navy that he was going to go home to Virginia while on leave. Actually, he was carrying classified materials with him on his way to the PRC to meet a PRC government employee. Lin was arrested in the Honolulu, Hawaii airport on his way to that meeting. He claimed he was going to meet a love interest, and he claimed it was social, even though she was a government employee of the PRC. It is worth noting again that the Chinese government requires by law that all Chinese citizens act as spies for the Chinese government at any and all times. We also know that Lin had contact with Taiwan's Republic of China Navy, and that he concealed those contacts.

Lin was charged with treason, knowingly mishandling classified documents, lying to his superior officers, and having unreported contacts with foreigners. The initial charge of treason against Lin could have resulted in him receiving the death penalty. After taking a plea bargain, Lin received a mere nine-year sentence, with the last three years suspended. Part of his plea was that he had to act as a cooperating witness. We cannot confirm how much information Lin actually passed to the PRC government or the government of Taiwan. Sadly, the Lin case is a great example of the fact that spending billions of our taxpayer cash to develop fantastic new technologies only makes sense when we don't leave all of that technology at the doorsteps of our nation's enemies.

Space is also a frontier for spy planes. The USAF is, appropriately, hush-hush about its X-37 program. The X-37, made by Boeing Defense, is an unmanned orbiter that can remain in space for many months at a time. It is smaller than NASA's manned space shuttles, but it does not require life support systems for crewmembers. Presumably, the X-37 would be able to bring its own large intelligence payload in its cargo bay to operate at any orbiting station. It would presumably also make possible the rapid placement and retrieval of satellites from a wide variety of orbits as needed. In other words, it could be stationed over Moscow at one moment and repositioned over Vladivostok an hour later. The possible capabilities for such a spacecraft are breathtaking and boggle the imagination. We hope that those capabilities remain in the realm of the imagination of foreign governments and not in their technical files. Thankfully, it appears that Boeing and the USAF have succeeded in guarding the X-37 design and technologies so far, and we salute them for that.

Another possible Air Force project is the rumored "Aurora Project." As far as the US DOD and USAF are concerned, no such project exists. Many claims have been made of radar and satellite tracks of a Mach 5+ cruising speed reconnaissance and/or light bomber aircraft flown from US and UK air bases. The craft supposedly has an exceedingly long range and a payload capacity comparable to the retired USAF SR-71. We hope those things are true, but in this instance, the DOD, USAF, and CIA are keeping their mouths shut. All we can do is speculate.

As indicated by this ongoing production, spy planes remain an important part of intelligence gathering. Since the end of the Cold War, the advent of ultra-sophisticated drones and improvements in satellite technologies have decreased the need for manned spy plane missions into denied airspace. Any current manned intelligence mission flights into enemy airspace remain highly classified. Perhaps in 2050 we will hear about exploits of spy plane crews from 2021. Until then, it's a safe bet that some unsung heroes are still risking more than just the usual mechanical problems and bad weather when they take to the air.

26

WHEN CHINA SPANKED VIETNAM

WHEN THOSE OF US IN THE WESTERN WORLD THINK OF THE COLD War, we generally remember it as a battle between capitalist democracies and the communist dictatorships of the Soviet Union, its satellite states, and the People's Republic of China. It's easy to forget that the Soviet Union and Communist China were not exactly swapping friendship bracelets and braiding each other's hair. They had their own skirmishes going, among them the Sino-Vietnamese War of 1979.

February 17 marks the anniversary of the Communist Chinese invasion of Vietnam. In Communist China, as in the rest of the world, that anniversary is ignored each year. In Vietnam, the communist government does not focus much attention on the anniversary, but many of the Vietnamese people that reside in the northernmost provinces commemorate the day with visits to the graves of family members that died during the 1979 Chinese invasion.

In the West, the Sino-Vietnamese War is largely misunderstood or simply forgotten. The most obvious question is, "Why did it happen?" How is it that fraternal communist states managed to go to war with each other in the midst of the Cold War between communist and capitalist nations?

The first part of the answer is that many fraternal communist states were not as fraternal as they wanted the world to believe. Vietnam and the PRC had never had warm relations. Vietnam saw its powerful neighbor to the north as a constant threat to its security and was leery of Chinese military assistance during the French-Indochinese War.

The Soviet Union and the PRC also failed to realize anything like fraternal warmth and were occasionally involved in military skirmishes along their shared border. As the French-Indochinese War played out, the Soviet Union and communist North Vietnam developed close relations, and the Soviet Union was the main provider of military and economic aid to North Vietnam. That close relationship continued during the American-Indochinese War.

When the United States abandoned Vietnam, the communist Vietnamese government wanted to consolidate communist revolutions in Laos and Cambodia under Vietnamese hegemony with support from, and allegiance to, the Soviet Union. The Vietnamese viewed this as the most obvious strategy for keeping the PRC out of Southeast Asia. Unfortunately for Vietnam, China had its own plans for Southeast Asia.

The modern PRC is fond of portraying itself as being something like a neutral and peace-loving country. It is quick to claim that it has never exported revolution. The inference is that, while the Soviets pursued imperialist aims, China was busy experiencing a joyous cultural revolution and building a better workers' paradise. The reality was that, unlike the Soviet Union, Communist China was simply unable to realize its own imperialist aspirations. That didn't keep it from trying.

While the communists in Vietnam were dealing with the United States in South Vietnam, the Chinese were building a Chinese-aligned communist regime in Cambodia. In 1975, with the help of China, genocidal maniac leader of the Khmer Rouge communist movement, Pol Pot, came to power in Cambodia. He renamed Cambodia "Kampuchea." Pol Pot consolidated his position, and, assured of full support from the PRC, he cut off relations with the communist regime in Hanoi.

Then, in 1976, the ruthless Communist Chinese dictator, Mao Zedong, finally succeeded in doing something positive for China. He died.

When the dust settled, a new and vastly more effective oligarchy led by Deng Xiaoping rose to power in Communist China. Deng had a better grip on reality than Mao ever had. Deng and his supporters grasped the concept of China as a big country in a bigger world, and he was more concerned by Soviet aggression.

On the surface, Deng's regime had to maintain a veneer of good old-fashioned communist hatred for capitalist demons, but in practice, the Chinese quickly began to emulate those "capitalist demons." Deng was not in love with capitalist philosophy, but he admired capitalist results and wanted to improve China's pathetic economy. Deng and his supporters were either unwilling or unable to substantially improve relations with the Soviet Union, and they quietly made overtures to the United States.

The PRC's continued support for the Pol Pot regime would seem inconsistent with the modernizations and limited liberalizations that were being implemented at home. However, Deng chose to ignore the Khmer Rouge's genocidal conduct because they were the one non-Soviet-controlled option in Cambodia.

In 1978, with the "filthy American imperialist dogs" gone and the South Vietnamese government vanquished, the Vietnamese decided to try their own hand at a bit of fun-filled filthy imperial-ism. They invaded Cambodia. The Soviet Union provided finan-cial and military support for the operation. The PRC was infuriated. The Chinese responded by reinforcing their military along their border with the Soviet Union.

Much of the Vietnamese Army was in Cambodia in 1979, chasing down Khmer Rouge forces and trying to install a Vietnamese-controlled government. Because of this, Deng's military leaders decided that the time was ripe to invade Vietnam.

The PRC military leadership correctly predicted that the Soviet Union would not attempt to invade or attack China because the Soviets needed to maintain their military focus against well-equipped NATO forces in Europe. The PRC military incorrectly predicted that Vietnam would quickly recall all of its troops from Cambodia to defend the motherland from the Chinese invasion, and that this would save the Khmer Rouge.

While visiting the United States in January of 1979, Deng Xiaoping told American President Jimmy Carter that, "The little child is getting naughty; it's time he be spanked." It was not a bluff. On February 17, 1979, the PRC invaded Vietnam. The details of that war, as with all wars, depend upon whom you ask.

The Vietnamese version of the story is that six hundred thousand of the PRC's best troops invaded Vietnam and raped, pillaged, and murdered women and children. Due to the superiority of the courageous Vietnamese local militia forces, the cowardly Chinese suffered massive casualties and were forced to retreat.

The Chinese version of the story differs a bit. They invaded politely with about 200,000 troops, quickly vanquished the Viet-namese, and, although the path to Hanoi was open, chose to be magnanimous in victory and withdrew from Vietnam.

The truth is that the PRC did mobilize 600,000 troops in Southern China, but only 200,000 crossed the border. Thanks to Soviet satellite imagery, the Vietnamese calculated that the Chinese lacked the required strength and logistical support to actually attack Hanoi. The Vietnamese did not withdraw all of their forces from Cambodia, and the Khmer Rouge did not regain control of Cambodia.

The Chinese suffered about 6500 hundred fatalities and perhaps fifteen thousand wounded. The PRC claimed to have counted 57,000 dead Vietnamese soldiers and 100,000 dead Vietnamese militia members. The Chinese claims are likely wildly exaggerated, but they may have counted the many unarmed Vietnamese civilians they killed as militia.

The PRC did not withdraw due to a manpower shortage. It withdrew because it lacked the logistical capability to continue the invasion. On their way home, the Chinese did their best to destroy anything useful in northern Vietnam. The PRC could easily tolerate the casualties in Vietnam, but it could not tolerate the economic costs. By March 16, 1979, the PRC's withdrawal was complete.

The Western media coverage of the war was mostly amateurish, somewhat creative, and often inaccurate. Media lacked enough sources in the war zone, but that didn't stop them from making wild assumptions. Many journalists focused on the theory that the US Intelligence Community had "failed completely" in predicting the Chinese invasion. The Intelligence Community hadn't failed at all. When Deng chatted with President Carter in January 1979, Carter told him that the United States was aware of the Chinese mobilizations in progress along the Vietnam border. Deng didn't deny it. He was frank with President Carter about his intentions.

As they usually do, the Western media assumed that, since the CIA had not reported anything to *them* about the Chinese buildup, it meant the agency was once again blindsided by world events. The media then, as now, was unable to fathom that the Director of the CIA reports to the US president, and now to the Director of National Intelligence, rather than to the press corps. What the president decides to tell the media is up to . . . the president.

In the aftermath of the war, Vietnam conducted reprisals against non-ethnic Vietnamese that were assumed to have supported the Chinese invasion. Thousands were killed, and tens of thousands were resettled to work camps in southern Vietnam. The economic damage that the PRC had inflicted had a long-lasting negative impact on the economy of northern Vietnam.

For their part, the Chinese instituted a modernization campaign of the military, but that modernization had to wait for the Chinese economy to recuperate from Mao's highly destructive "cultural revolution." Only after decades of highly profitable trade with capitalist Western nations has that long-awaited military modernization finally come to fruition in China.

In 1979, the Vietnamese loathed and feared the Chinese, but today, they fear the more powerful, modernized PRC even more. The 1979 Chinese invasion of Vietnam was not the first. It may well not be the last.

27

BRINGING DOWN THE COSA NOSTRA

THE COLD WAR BATTLE BETWEEN THE SOVIET AND CHINESE communists and the capitalist free world penetrated the lives of billions in countries around the globe. Americans grew up with nuclear war drills, the space race to beat the Soviets, and kissing their drafted loved ones good-bye, sometimes for forever, to fight on foreign shores for reasons they did not fully understand. And though the struggle between capitalism and communism was certainly the overriding theme of the Cold War Era, other significant wars were waged far from the backstreets of Paris and Berlin and the battlefields of Korea and Vietnam. One of those was the war against the Sicilian Mafia.

After the decline of the Sicilian feudal system in 1812, powerful regional crime groups took root throughout Sicily. A variety of claims about the origin of the Cosa Nostra have been put forth. Depending upon whom we listen to, the Mafia can be traced to anywhere from rural Sicilian land owners of the late 1700s to secretive Arabic gangs from before the time of Christ. Regardless of the lack of agreement concerning its birth, by the 20th century, the Mafia had amassed tremendous power and wealth across

Sicily, and it had exported its crime franchises across the United States, Canada, Australia, and parts of South America. Inside Sicily, individual Mafia gangs were organized along territorial borders.

In the 1930s, when heroin supplies from China and Japan dwindled due to the war raging in Asia, heroin labs opened in Sicily and in the area around the port city of Marseilles, France. In Sicily, the Mafia used its growing heroin profits to influence government and insulate itself from the law. That influence grew to crippling proportions.

Crime and corruption mushroomed, and a seemingly endless series of murders paralyzed Sicily. The Mafia appeared omnipotent, and fear of it prevented the Italian government from acquiring enough witnesses to prosecute those murders. A succession of Italian governments made attempts to curtail the Sicilian Mafia and other organized crime systems in Italy, but their success was limited. Immense wealth coupled with a multi-generational membership system made Italian organized crime groups nearly impossible to penetrate. The decent people of Sicily desperately needed champions—extraordinary people who were strong enough and brave enough to break the back of the all-powerful Mafia. Many heard the call and answered, and among the bravest who stepped up to the fight was Judge Paolo Borsellino.

Paolo Borsellino was born in Palermo on January 19, 1940, at a time when Benito Mussolini and his fascist party were at war with the Sicilian "Cosa Nostra." Borsellino came from a working class family. During his youth, poverty racked Sicily, and education was difficult to obtain, but Borsellino managed to attend Palermo University. During his University days, Paolo befriended like-minded youths, and he joined the right wing Fronte Universitario d'Azione Nazionale. Through this student political group,

Borsellino formed long-lasting relationships with men who he could trust in his later battle against the Mafia.

Paolo persevered in his studies, and, in 1962, he graduated from the law school at Palermo with honors. In 1963, he passed the judicial exam and was assigned to various courts throughout Sicily until his return to Palermo in 1968. The humble native son returned to his birthplace with the intention of restoring Palermo, and all of Sicily, to its rightful owners—the honest working people of Sicily. No normal man or average judge would have started such a fight. Fortunately for Italy, Paolo Borsellino was neither a normal man nor an average judge. Along with his trusted colleagues—Prosecutor Rocco Chinnici and Magistrate Giovanni Falcone—Borsellino organized an elite anti-Mafia crime fighting unit. Handpicked Carabinieri with distinguished records were assigned to the task force.

Readers might wonder why these men didn't expect the powerful Sicilian Mafia to target them. Actually, they did. The task force was formed with the intention of passing institutional knowledge of the Mafia from one generation to the next, no matter how short a generation's tenure might be. These men assumed that they would eventually pay with their lives for what they were doing. Though they knew they would not survive the war, they wanted the war to survive their passing. The group formulated a massive body of history and current knowledge about the Mafia.

New members of the task force were surprised and sometimes frustrated at the time they had to spend studying the history of the Mafias of Sicily before they were allowed to become active in operations, but when seasoned Carabinieri entered the battle against the forces of the Mafia with a more complete intelligence assessment, they knew who was who. They knew who the gang members' ancestors were, what the borders of the gangs were, and what methods the gangs had and did use. Most importantly, they trusted the men they fought with and the prosecutors and judges for whom they worked.

In the late 1960s, as the task force began to rack up victories against the wealthy and powerful Mafioso groups of Sicily, a new factor emerged in the war against the Sicilian Mafia. A hitherto insignificant Mafia faction from rural Corleone, led by Salvatore "Totò" Riina and Bernardo Provenzano, started making inroads into the lucrative streets of Palermo. The Palermo Mafia families apparently underestimated the determination and ruthlessness of the new leaders of the Corleone Mafia. That underestimation would cost them their lives.

Provenzano used patient tactics and preferred to remain in the background. The brash Riina wanted to use terror to gain power. The Corleonesi carefully crafted strong alliances with other, less powerful families, and then they proceeded to wreak havoc in Palermo. Their campaign of murder against officials and rival families was designed to implicate or intimidate the Palermo families. It was effective in weakening the Palermo families and keeping the Anti-Mafia Task Force busy chasing them.

The Carabinieri estimate that from 1980 to 1983, a period known in Sicily as the Second Mafia War, the Corleonesi Mafia was responsible for the murders of at least a thousand people. Those murders included Carabinieri, magistrates, prosecutors, and innocent children. As the old Mafia establishment of Palermo crumbled, Riina and Provenzano picked up the pieces. Within four years, they were able to gain control of the lucrative Palermo heroin export. But Riina and Provenzano miscalculated, just as their victims had. A particularly popular and highly respected Carabinieri by the name of General Carlo Dalla Chiesa was summoned to reinforce the task force. On May 1, 1982, during the height of the Second Mafia War, the general became prefect of Palermo.

Carlo Alberto Dalla Chiesa had earned the adoration of Italy and the trust of the US intelligence establishment because of his outstanding success against the Italian Red Brigade terrorist group. When the Red Brigade had kidnapped US Army General James Dozier on December 16, 1981, the Italian government rejected offers of help from President Reagan, but the White House, the Pentagon, and the CIA did not trust Italy to act with alacrity and integrity. The United States dispatched its own hand-picked operatives to "assist" in the Italian manhunt. The United States did not expect those operatives to ask for permission from Italy.

One of the young members of that group decided to take the risk of reaching out directly to Dalla Chiesa. It was his judgment that Dalla Chiesa could be trusted. It was Dalla Chiesa's judgment that the US intruders who had appeared from outside of normal channels could be trusted. An alliance was quietly formed, and, thanks to the hard work and courage of the Carabinieri, General Dozier was recovered alive.

When Dalla Chiesa arrived in Sicily, he efficiently deployed new manpower and the pressure on the Mafia increased with frequent arrests. Mobster Totò Riina decided that the war against the government of Italy should be expanded to teach them a lesson.

On September 3, 1982, General Carlo Alberto Dalla Chiesa, his wife, and his bodyguard were ambushed and murdered in Palermo. Italy lost a great and honest leader, but unfortunately for Riina, Provenzano, and the Corleone crime machine, the people of Sicily did not respond with the anticipated fear. Sicilians protested against the Mafia and the Italian government's corruption. Members of the US Intelligence Community did not forget the honest general who had kept his word. It is rumored that after the death of Carlo Dalla Chiesa, the United States offered various resources to the Anti-Mafia Task Force in Sicily outside of formal channels.

Riina didn't back down. On July 29, 1983, the new Task Force leader, Rocco Chinnici, and two bodyguards were murdered by a car bomb. The people of Sicily didn't back down. The war continued.

Then a crack began to form in Totò Riina's armor. Tommaso Buscetta, a member of one of the families Riina had nearly wiped out, decided that it was time to stop Riina. Because of his rage against Riina, Buscetta agreed to turn against the Mafia, and he became one of the most valuable informants ever in the war against the Mafia.

In 1986, with the help of Buscetta's testimony, Prosecutor Giovanni Falcone and Judge Paolo Borsellino were able to obtain convictions and long sentences against 350 Sicilian Mafioso. It was the greatest single hammer blow of all time against the Sicilian Mafia. Several mob families collapsed as a result of the mass convictions, but Riina and Provenzano remained at large. Judge Borsellino knew that he was living on borrowed time.

On July 19, 1992, that time came due. Judge Paolo Borsellino and five police body guards—Agostino Catalano, Walter Cosina, Emanuela Loi, Vincenzo Li Muli, and Claudio Traina—were murdered by a car bomb in Palermo, Sicily.

The Italian public reacted with sustained outrage. They had had enough, and they wanted their country back. For the first time, Sicilians brazenly defied the Mafia as their rage overcame their fear. They posted large signs on homes and businesses demanding the death of the Mafia. On January 15, 1993, the Carabinieri finally captured and arrested Totò Riina in Palermo. After twenty-three years as a fugitive, Riina was condemned to multiple life sentences.

Many believe that Bernardo Provenzano had grown tired of Riina's bloody direct attack against the government and judicial system of Italy, and that Provenzano tipped off the task force with Riina's whereabouts. Holmes is among those believers. So was Totò Riina. Riina's arrest was followed by the arrests of his closest assistants and the collapse of Riina's violent reign.

With Riina out of the way, Provenzano lived on the run and avoided the opulence preferred by his old cohort Riina. He usually hid in sheepherder shacks and cabins in rural mountain areas, relying on a cautious messenger system to rule the Sicilian Mafia from afar with far less noise and violence than what marked the Riina reign. Few Mafia bosses were granted even brief face time with him, and even his wife and two sons did not see him for years. Provenzano pleaded with the various families to avoid violence, lecturing that, in the wake of Riina's bloody massacres, the people of Sicily would not tolerate open mob violence.

In 2006, the Carabinieri began to close in on Bernardo Provenzano after the capture of a messenger. Two waves of arrests netted over one hundred Mafiosi in the Corleone area, but not Provenzano. Finally, on April 11, 2006, after over four decades on the run, Bernardo Provenzano was captured when an alert Carabinieri team tailed a delivery of medicine and fresh clothes sent to him from Corleone.

Provenzano was transferred to the Ultimate Maximum Security Penitentiary known as Hell on July 13, 2016, and Riina joined him there on November 17, 2017. To Provenzano's credit, while Riina's two sons are sharing their father's fate and serving life sentences, Provenzano had learned enough about Mafia life to want his sons to take no part in it, and his sons have never been suspected of any crime beyond speeding tickets.

Hundreds of Mafioso remain in maximum security prison. A man who Holmes admired and trusted, General Carlo Alberto Dalla Chiesa, is long dead. He has not been forgotten. Prosecutor Giovanni Falcone, Judge Paolo Borsellino, and dozens of other prosecutors, judges, and honest Carabinieri and policemen are gone. Dozens of innocent bystanders, including an eleven-year-old boy who was tortured and strangled to death by Riina's goons, are gone. But something remains.

The people of Sicily know that there are men and women who will not be bought or cowered by the vermin in the Mafia or any other criminal gang. They found their voice. They have not lost it. There is still a Mafia, and there will always be corruption, but as long as the sacrifices of men and women like Paolo Borsellino are remembered, evil will likely never be allowed to openly rule the people of Sicily again.

A memorial olive tree is planted in Via d'Amelio, Palermo, to commemorate Paolo Borsellino's sacrifice. At the base of the tree is a plaque that reads, "You that come here to regard, remember: not all Sicilians are Mafiosi and not all Mafiosi are Sicilians."

28

THAT DAMNED BERLIN WALL

ON A COLD, JANUARY DAY IN 1961, IN A WORLD CHILLED BY THE threat of nuclear Armageddon, Holmes sat near a radio with his family and listened intently to the words of the new president of his country, John Fitzgerald Kennedy—words that told him that his freedom came not from government, but from God. The new president told him that every nation, whether they wish us well or wish us ill, should know "that we shall pay any price, bear any burden, meet any hardship, support any friend, oppose any foe, to assure the survival and the success of liberty." Holmes hears those words still.

Few words have influenced his life or the world as those words did. Millions of people around the world also heard, and some found hope and assurance. Others heard those words as a challenge to their right to take freedom from others.

Seven months later, the Soviet Union erected a wall between the Soviet-controlled sector of Berlin and the Western-controlled sector of Berlin. Situated deep inside Soviet-occupied East Germany, West Berlin was a beacon of hope surrounded by a sea of Soviet oppression.

By 1961, nearly four million Germans living under Soviet occupation decided to abandon their homes and seek freedom in West
Germany. The easiest place to cross from East Germany to West
Germany was Berlin. One night in August of 1961, the Soviet and
East German troops formed a cordon along the dividing line
between East and West Berlin, and the next day, they began to
erect a concrete wall to deter any more freedom seekers.

Streets and buildings were removed from the east side of the wall
to create a killing zone. East Germans, under the control of the
Soviet Union, built fences topped with barbed wire and guard
towers equipped with machine guns. Like a monster from some
cheap science fiction movie, the Wall grew taller and wider over
time, as if it were growing fat on the flesh of the nearly two
hundred East Germans who were murdered while trying to
cross it.

The Soviets congratulated themselves for the effectiveness of the
Wall in stemming the tide of escapees from the Soviet police
state. The West saw it as a shameful monument to totalitarianism
and an open admission by the Soviets that, given the opportunity,
any sane man or woman would seek freedom over oppression.

During the Cold War, the great central debate between the
Soviet- and Maoist- controlled East and the West centered, in
theory, on the struggle between communism and capitalism.
Some of our generation debated the appeal of "Marxism" vs.
"Capitalism," but whatever Marx might have said didn't matter.
He was long gone, and his ideas weren't deciding policy in
Moscow. How the Soviets divided their land or ran their economy
did not make as much of an impression on our generation as that
damned Berlin Wall. The men, women, and children who were
murdered trying to cross it said everything there was to say about
Soviet communism, and their deaths were all we needed to know
about which side of the Wall we preferred to live on.

In the East, the Warsaw Pact had over 3.6 million troops facing west and south. In Western and Southern Europe, NATO countered that with 3.7 million troops. Surrounded as it was by East Germany, the view east from West Berlin was much less comforting. In West Berlin, approximately 10,000 allied troops, known in the United States as the Berlin Brigade, were surrounded by 250,000 Warsaw Pact troops. Outnumbered or not, the Berlin Brigade did not intend to ever surrender if war returned to Berlin.

The Berlin Wall remained a symbol of the political dynamic between East and West for twenty-eight years. In June of 1987, Ronald Reagan visited the Brandenburg Gate, and at the same place that John Kennedy had delivered his famous Berlin speech within sight of the Wall, Reagan delivered a speech. In response to reformist Soviet President Mikhail Gorbachev's claims that the Soviet Union sought peace and prosperity, he challenged Gorbachev to, "Tear down this wall!"

In August of 1989, unwilling Soviet "ally" Hungary opened its border between Hungary and Austria. Thousands of East Germans and other Eastern Europeans escaped to the West via Hungary. The Soviets pressured Hungary to stop the escaping Eastern Europeans. Hungary pretended to comply, but looked for opportunities to defy its KGB taskmasters. Protests began in East Germany, and East Germans began to chant, "We want to leave." Each week, the protests grew in strength.

In October of 1989, the longtime East German General Secretary Erich Honecker, who had elevated brown-nosing Moscow to an art form at the expense of the German people, resigned and was replaced by a slightly less homicidal maniac named Egon Krenz. On the occasion of his retirement, Honecker announced to the world that the Berlin Wall would remain for at least another fifty years.

East and West Berliners began to congregate at the Wall, and the protests continued to grow. Krenz had been offered up as a reformist, but East Germans recognized him for what he was—a ruthless, self-promoting politician who was, in fact, attempting to crack down on reformers in his own government. The East German military began to show signs of mutiny. Krenz was quickly becoming a puppet king without a kingdom, and East Germany had over $100 billion in debt with no way to make payments.

Buried under deep layers of its own cynicism and impaired by factional maneuvering, the Soviet Politburo was busy with its own internal struggles, and it had little inclination to reinforce East Germany with cash or Soviet troops. Krenz was making fast progress on the road to nowhere. His Polish and Czechoslovak allies to the east had slipped the Soviet leash, and he was beginning to understand what the Berlin Brigade must have felt like for so long.

East German protesters changed their chant from "We want to leave" to "We want to stay. *You* leave!"

By November, it was becoming obvious that most of the East German border guards were sympathetic to the opposition. With a possible collapse of the government looming, nobody in the East German government wanted to have to answer for ordering a slaughter of the ever-more-brazen protestors. On November 9, 1989, in an attempt to relieve the social pressure that was threatening to rupture the East German state, the East German government announced that the gates would be opened in the Wall, and that anyone who wished could pass from East to West.

Until late October, Holmes had been in Europe. On his flight back to Washington, DC, he wondered if his dream of seeing a free Eastern Europe was about to materialize. The Soviet steamroller that had kept Eastern Europe's puppet communist regimes in power for four decades had run out of steam. On November 9, he returned home from a martial arts class. When he entered the living room, his wife was smiling in a way that he had not seen her smile before. She said, "You got your wish," and she pointed to the TV.

Holmes felt compelled to get close to the screen, as though he could hug the Berliners who were dancing on top of that damned Wall. He wished he had gone back to Berlin, as he missed the biggest party in the history of the Cold War.

He was stunned and relieved and simultaneously filled with joy and sadness. He felt joy for the people of Eastern Europe and for us in the West. In that moment, he couldn't help but wish that a few people who mattered greatly to him could have remained among us long enough to see that night. They had paid that price. They had borne that burden. It had not been in vain. He never for a second thought that it would be.

Tonight, from the distant, warm, comfortable safety of our homes, we offer our humble gratitude to those who were lost in the fight for never losing their faith, and to the people of Berlin and Eastern Europe for finding their faith and their freedom.

29

VLADIMIR PUTIN—LIVING LEGACY OF THE KGB

"Whoever does not miss the Soviet Union has no heart. Whoever wants it back has no brain." ~ Widely attributed to Vladimir Putin, but as with most things Putin, it's debatable.

THE DAY AFTER CHRISTMAS IN 1991, HOLMES RECEIVED A Christmas present that he had long worked for and often wished for, but never quite expected—the Soviet police state dissolved. Being the incurable optimist that he is, Holmes wondered how much freedom and reform the people of Russia and their captive states would manage to clutch before chaos and crime infringed on their long-awaited honeymoon with democracy. Sadly, his question was answered all too soon.

In May of 2000, when Russian President Boris Yeltsin resigned from office, a "new" face burst onto the international political scene with a sudden flash, and that bright light has yet to dim. That face was Vladimir Putin, the one-time KGB counterintelligence officer and Leningrad political golden boy. The face was new to the Western media, but not to Russian political insiders.

As recycled KGB functionaries go, Vlady has always been adept at catching a front seat on whatever political bandwagon is able to free its wheels from the morass of deep, cold mud that constitutes post-Soviet Russian politics. While so much of the Russian political world seems to crawl at a snail's pace, Putin can usually be found racing ahead with confidence. By the time he became the President of Russia in 2000, he had plenty of experience in political intrigue.

Putinologists of various stripes don't all agree on Putin's biography and family history. As with so much of history, Vlady's early years are hard to pin down. Since he was KGB, there isn't much public information to dig up, and before he was famous, nobody really cared about him, so nothing was written about him prior to him becoming Boris Yeltsin's Director of the Federal Security Service in July of 1998. Also, the job of ferreting out Vlady's early days is made more difficult by the fact that Team Putin continues to scrub what there is on his relatively unremarkable youth and replace it with something more like what one would expect if Hercules and a factory worker had a baby.

The fog around Putin's beginnings begins at his beginnings. The current, widely-promoted story is that Putin was the child of factory workers Vladimir Putin and Maria Shelomova in St. Petersburg, and that his family shared an apartment with two other families. He supposedly was late to join the Red Pioneers and the Communist Party.

Is this true? We can't say. We do know "factory worker" and "late to embrace communism" are popular yarns for politicians to spin in Russia these days as they try to be "men of the people." In other words, Russian politicians are just like American politicians. When it is profitable for them to do so, those who have led privileged, elitist lives play down their upper-class backgrounds by adopting foreign accents . . . like Southern . . . and telling stories of picking lettuce with migrant workers. It's said there are two certainties in life, but there are actually three: death, taxes, and the lies of politicians.

The version some Putinologists recall from two decades ago was that Putin's parents were both KGB, that they didn't share an apartment with anyone, and that Vlady was a typical and rather unremarkable Red Brigade kid who grew up to follow in his parents' footsteps in the Communist Party and the KGB. Except for Putin being KGB and a Party member, this recollection is difficult to back up. That's because, like so many things on the internet in Russia, China, America, and everywhere else on the planet, they disappear from public record when they become inconvenient to people in power, so categorically, we can neither confirm nor deny this version of Vlady's early social status.

There is yet another story of Putin's beginnings, and this one is an Obama-style birther story. Vera Putina from the Metekhi, 18 miles from Gory in the Georgia region, claims Putin is *her* son. She says Vlady's father is a Georgian mechanic who got her pregnant while he was married to another woman. She had Vladimir and married a Georgian soldier who wanted her to get rid of the boy, so she sent him to his grandparents in Russia. Then, Vladimir Putin and Maria Shelomova, in their forties and childless after both their sons died, adopted Vlady.

The evidence supporting this version is that a Vladimir Putin was registered at an elementary school in the village of Metekhi from 1959–1960. Also, an old schoolteacher from Metekhi claims Vladimir Putin was her student. She also claims she was threatened and told to keep her mouth shut. In addition, some Russian birthers point to the fifteen-year gap between Vladimir's birth and that of his older deceased brother as evidence that Vlady was adopted.

It's worth noting that a Russian journalist working on this story died in a plane crash, and an Italian journalist, Antonio Russo, supposedly was onto something just before he was murdered. Vera Putina wants DNA tests run, but that's not happening.

This is of interest not only because it's interesting, but, as in the Obama birther debate, it would mean that Vlady would have been born in Georgia, not Russia, and, therefore, would not legally be permitted to be President of Russia.

In yet another twist, some believe that Putin's mother, Maria Shelomova, was Jewish, and that Putin is in a vast conspiracy with Jews. . . . We've got nothing on that one beyond common sense and history indicating otherwise.

As varied as these stories are, some purported facts are consistent about Putin's early years. The parents who raised him were Vladimir Putin and Maria Shelomova. He had two older brothers that he never met, Albert and Viktor, one of whom died of diphtheria, and the other who died in infancy. Vlady attended school at Primary School #193 on Boskov Lane in St. Petersburg from 1960–1968, and then attended High School #281. He was supposedly outstanding in math and science.

Some reports claim Putin started studying martial arts in high school, and some say he was a martial arts expert by the time he got there. Also, it was once common to see people who knew Putin in elementary school and high school on interviews saying Putin was a cold, quiet, unfriendly child who had no friends. Those quotes have mostly vanished. We don't know whether or not the people who gave those quotes have also vanished. In 1970, Putin entered Leningrad State University to study law, and he joined the Communist Party while he was a student there. At some point, he entered the KGB.

In 1983, Putin married Lyudmila Putina. They had two daughters, Marya and Yekaterina, and then divorced in 2014. Putin does not discuss his children, and they are heavily guarded.

Not one to wait for his political car to sink too deeply into that infamous Russian mud, Putin began working quietly for the mayor of Leningrad in the spring of 1990 while still a KGB officer. Ever the capable and ambitious pragmatist, he resigned his KGB position when the Soviet Union filed for political bankruptcy and began openly working for the Leningrad city government as a political adviser on international affairs. Score one for Vlady's foresight.

Putin was appointed head of the Leningrad Committee for Foreign Investment in June of 1991. By the summer of 1992, he was under investigation by the Leningrad Legislative Committee for an alleged kickback scheme from the underpriced export of Russian metals. The Committee requested that the mayor fire Putin, but Putin remained in office. He was apparently already something of an untouchable, or he at least knew enough to share the profits with the right people.

Post-Soviet Russia's descent into chaos began. Petyr Baelish says in the Game of Thrones series, "Chaos isn't a pit. Chaos is a ladder. . . . Only the ladder is real. The climb is all there is." George R.R. Martin must have had Vladimir Putin in mind when he wrote that line, because no one is better at climbing the ladder of Chaos.

In June of 1996, Putin became Deputy Director for Presidential Property Management. The title sounds like a name for the head caretaker of the president's residence, but with that innocent title came the power to control Russia's foreign assets. Putin was in charge of transferring the property of the old Soviet Union from state control to private control in the supposedly free market economy of the new Russian state. Some say that many of those assets ended up in his own hands.

A mere two years later in 1998, Russian President Boris Yeltsin appointed Putin Director of the FSB, which is roughly the Russian version of the Soviet KGB. Putin was experienced KGB, and Yeltzin wanted an insider, his *own* insider, in the office. Then, in August of 1999, President Yeltsin appointed Putin as one of Russia's three deputy prime ministers. Before the month was out, Putin climbed the Ladder of Chaos to the office of Prime Minister of Russia.

Putin wasted no time. In a roiling political climate, he orchestrated an effective crackdown on the separatist rebels in Chechnya in Central Russia. He also organized a loud and well-filmed campaign against corruption that was likely more drama than substance. The giant public relations scheme was effective. Putin's power grew.

Boris Yeltsin had polished his own image as a democratic reformer during the post-Soviet years, but he and his family came under investigation for corruption charges in the winter of 1999 with allegations that Yeltsin was embezzling from a major Russian state-sponsored construction project. That investigation was led by Russian Chief Prosecutor Yury Skuratov, who spoke more publicly and with confidence. In December of 1999, the ailing Boris Yeltsin stepped down, and Prime Minister Vladimir Putin became the Acting President of Russia.

Skuratov was told that authorities had obtained a video of him having a ménage-a-trois with two young women. Skuratov responded with a scoff. Three months later, in March of 2000, the video aired on state-controlled Russian TV. Few people actually believed the man in the video was Skuratov. However, in April,

Putin and the Russian Interior Minister held a press conference. Vlady declared that the FSB had investigated, and that the FSB's "expert analysis" had confirmed that the mystery man in the video was, indeed, Prosecutor Yury Skuratov. Putin claimed that the sexual encounter was paid for by criminals under investigation by Skuratov's office. Though many did not believe this story, this "revelation" was enough to derail the prosecution of Boris Yeltsin.

As Acting President of Russia, Putin continued to build his image and his power. A dedicated atheist and sworn oppressor of religious expression under the Soviets, Putin began pushing the notion that he was actually a devout Russian Orthodox Catholic all along, and that he had just hidden it well. In fact, Putin then took a public hand in negotiating a reunification of European and Russian branches of the resurgent Russian Orthodox churches. Remember folks, a vote for Putin is a vote for God.

To be fair, not all of Putin's efforts have gone toward self-aggrandizement. Once in office, he signed a decree protecting Boris Yeltsin and his family members from prosecution. Perhaps inspired by the possibilities should his own star begin to fall, two months later, Putin passed a law protecting *all* ex-presidents from prosecution. Why let Yeltsin have all the fun?

Not content to be the savior of the Russian Orthodox Catholic Church, Putin also designed his image around the theme of a Russian nationalist resurgence, vowing to rebuild Russia into a world superpower. He instituted a flat tax system that met with a popular response in Russia. Then, as gas and oil prices rose, Putin streamlined Russian efforts to complete new oil and gas projects for the sale of fossil fuels to the energy-hungry European markets. In return, those high oil and gas prices financed more Putin popularity as they fueled economic growth in Russia.

A great public relations campaign with state-run media never hurts a person's popularity, either. Stop for a moment, if you will, and remember the pictures you may have seen of Vladimir Putin during his tenure as Russian president from 2000 to 2008, as prime minister from 2008 to 2012, and again as president from 2012 until the present. These are a few of our personal favorites:

- Well-orchestrated photo ops with his competing world leaders from Bush to the aging Castro.
- Heart-warming appearances of Putin the churchgoer to admire.
- "Putin the brilliant underwater archaeologist" photos
- Putin the bad-ass biker
- And let's not forget Putin the tank driver, Putin the bomber pilot, and Putin the judo expert.

And those are just the ones that aren't photo shopped. He was also named Time Magazine's 2007 Person of the Year. Right now, we're thinking someone should drive Putin by a cancer research center and see if his fleeting proximity doesn't miraculously uncover a cure, or at least make the research center sparkle brightly for a while.

Putin's long campaign to "eliminate corruption" has also been well-publicized. It seems obvious to most who do not admire Putin that the campaign was a device for shifting power away from opposing oligarchs and their political gangs to himself and his backers.

At this point, we and most rational people not living under Putin's gun believe he owns significant shares of several Russian energy companies and armament industries, valued at several billion dollars. Putin, himself, sometimes claims his only income is from his government salary, and at other times he admits to being a founder of United Aircraft Corporation and of Gazprom, which is the world's largest single-entity* oil producer, holding the world's largest reserves of natural gas. Although Vlady claims to be just another overworked and underpaid Russian, more evidence has emerged that he is also the beneficiary of accounts at Swiss holding companies. In fact, some Putinologists say that Putin is the richest man in the world when his hidden assets are included in the tally. We'll leave it to you to decide what you think on that matter.

As for Putin's image abroad, it depends on who you ask. Dictators like Maduro in Venezuela and Assad in Syria think he's the best, as Russia is their avid supporter. Putin also supports Iran with military armaments and plenty of diplomatic backing for the mullahs' dreams of the Iranian Global Caliphate. Putin does his best to pal up to dictator Erdogan in Turkey, as well, driving a wedge into the NATO countries. Erdogan often takes the bait, but the two tyrants frequently have divergent interests so they aren't braiding each other's hair quite yet.

And America? Putin enjoyed a kinder, gentler image in the United States during the Obama era, with Obama making jokes about the 80s wanting their foreign policy back when others referred to Russia as the Main Enemy. Today, people are more aware of what has long been true—that with Putin at the helm, "Russia" is nothing more than the acronym for the Reorganized Union of Soviet Socialists In Asia, just without any pretense of socialism or communism.

Not all Russians are buying Putin's brighter, shinier Russia sales job. Many educated Russians are taking their educations and their entrepreneurial skills to Europe and North America, and some of those educated Russians have expressed a fear that human rights will continue to decline under Putin.

The precise truth in all this doesn't matter much in geopolitical terms, but the image does matter. Putin as the great Russian military leader, crime fighter, and economic whiz kid, along with virtually unlimited power to rig elections, is likely to assure he is elected to any office he wants for as long as he wants it. Regardless of whatever confusion we may have about Putin's record or his assets, we can be sure that he runs the show. The old stone-faced Soviet strong man, Leonid Brezhnev, would be jealous.

---

*The United States and Saudi Arabia both produce more oil than Russia, but in the United States and Saudi Arabia, multiple entities produce that oil. Gazprom is the world's largest single-entity oil producer.

IN CONCLUSION

One of the most important lessons military and intelligence professionals as well as civilians can learn is the great paradox of history—that history is both the foundation of all that is happening today as well as the mystery of our past that we will never fully resolve. As the wheel of time turns, facts morph into legends, legends into myths, and myths into ideologies as the societies of today recreate history in their own image to serve the present agendas born of the ignorance and vanity of this moment in time.

Each generation is convinced it has the corner on some original truth, unconceivable to the thousands of generations past. Each generation judges its forebears with the harsh eye of hubris, telling itself that it is morally superior, more justified, and more righteous, even as it commits the same failings and transgressions. Each individual generation is doomed to be humbled by experience as it ages, and eventually to be condemned by its progeny as the unending cycle of history repeats, the human race changing not over years, but only over eons.

We can only hope to break this cycle as individuals by setting aside our preconceived notions and filters and listening to the voices of the past without judgment on our part. If we are to learn from this past, we must relinquish the self-aggrandizing belief that we, unlike any previous generation, have today in 20/20 focus, with an understanding not afforded our ancestors.

It's easy to look back at the fragments of history and see how events were twisted and bowed to political forces in the past. What is not so easy is to see that history fragments the moment it is created—right now, today—splintered and subdued to serve the agendas of today's rulers, political forces, and societies, and that our "truth" of today is already sullied by the vanity and aims of humankind. Studying history reveals the trends and forces that shatter truths and how political forces reshape them so that we can then look at the pieces of our present with new eyes and push that eventual progress as a species.

In the meantime, almost everything that has ever happened is happening somewhere today. Almost everything that is happening today has happened before. Let that be our lesson.

PHOTO GALLERY

Visit our photo gallery with illustrations of some of the
individuals and events referenced in this book at our website,
BayardandHolmes.com.

ACKNOWLEDGMENTS

Our deepest gratitude to Vicki Hinze, Doug Patteson, John Cladianos, and the numerous contacts around the world who provided assistance in the compiling and publishing of this work.

Our humble indebtedness to our families for their tolerance of our late-night conversations and absenteeism to collaborate on this project.

Our abiding thanks to all of the dedicated professionals who gave us their time and efforts in the review and editing process.

Our undying appreciation to our readers. You make our efforts worthwhile.

Thank you, one and all.

ACKNOWLEDGMENTS

KEY FIGURES IN ESPIONAGE
THE GOOD, THE BAD, & THE BOOTY

KEY FIGURES IN ESPIONAGE IS A COLLECTION OF BRIEF BIOGRAPHIES of legendary heroes, infamous traitors, and courageous operatives who fought with their brilliance, their cunning, and their determination to succeed.

Using information gleaned from historical documents, original US military and intelligence documents, individuals and official records throughout allied countries, as well as personal experience, Bayard & Holmes reveal the fascinating lives of espionage greats like Billy Waugh and Virginia Hall, notorious turncoats like Robert Hanssen and Kim Philby, and brilliant operatives who used what their mamas gave them, such as Josephine Baker and Amy Thorpe. With dry humor and a digestible narrative style, this compilation both illuminates and informs.

"Key Figures in Espionage is a rollicking ride through some of history's most famous espionage personalities."

~ Doug Patteson, Film Advisor and Former CIA Operations Officer

Available at BayardandHolmes.com/nonfiction.

KEY PEOPLE & WARS
ASTONISHING INDIVIDUALS & CRUCIAL CONFLICTS

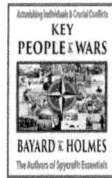

KEY PEOPLE & WARS IS A COLLECTION OF SHORT BIOGRAPHIES OF important Western military and intelligence figures and brief histories of critical conflicts that have helped shape the modern world.

From the founder of Special Forces, the would-be King of Mexico, and the man who taught the FBI to shoot, to the Battle of Manila, the Boer Wars, the Battle of Fallujah and more, Bayard & Holmes bring fifty years of military and intelligence experience to their narrative style to illuminate the heroes and events of the past that laid foundation for the world dynamics of today.

"When it comes to research into the clandestine depths of spycraft, the dynamic duo of Bayard & Holmes have put together a must-read series that is written with authority and is easily digestible.

~ James Rollins, #1 New York Times Bestselling Author

Available at BayardandHolmes.com/nonfiction.

PRAISE FOR BAYARD & HOLMES

"*Key Figures in Espionage* is a rollicking ride through some of history's most notorious espionage personalities. Well researched and written, the deep dive in to the Cambridge Five is particularly interesting. This book is great for not only the casual reader or spy fan but also for those who are more well versed in the subjects."

— DOUG PATTESON, FORMER CIA
OPERATIONS OFFICER

"When it comes to research into the clandestine depths of spycraft, the dynamic duo of Bayard & Holmes have put together a must-read series that is written with authority, yet easily digestible. I've already added their books to my shelf of writing essentials—you should, too!"

— JAMES ROLLINS, #1 NEW YORK TIMES
BESTSELLER OF *CRUCIBLE*

DESIGN

COVER and LAYOUT
by Piper Bayard

www.ingramcontent.com/pod-product-compliance
Lightning Source LLC
LaVergne TN
LVHW051044080426
835508LV00019B/1687